Canadian Living

150 ESSENTIAL

SALADS

TRANSCONTINENTAL BOOKS
5800 Saint-Denis St.
Suite 900
Montreal, Que. H2S 3L5

Telephone: 514-273-1066
Toll-free: 1-800-565-5531

canadianliving.com

Bibliothèque et Archives nationales du
Québec and Library and Archives Canada
cataloguing in publication

Main entry under title :
150 Essential Salads
"Canadian living".
Includes index.
ISBN 978-1-927632-02-4
1. Salads. 2. Cookbooks. I. Canadian Living
Test Kitchen.

TX740.S242 2014   641.83
C2014-940319-4

Project editor: Tina Anson Mine
Copy editor: Lisa Fielding
Indexer: Beth Zabloski
Art director: Colin Elliott

Printed in Canada
© Transcontinental Books, 2014
Legal deposit – 2nd quarter 2014
National Library of Quebec
National Library of Canada
ISBN 978-1-927632-02-4

We acknowledge the financial support of our
publishing activity by the Government of
Canada through the Canada Book Fund.

For information on special rates for
corporate libraries and wholesale purchases,
please call **1-866-800-2500**.

Canadian Living

150 ESSENTIAL

SALADS

BY THE CANADIAN LIVING TEST KITCHEN

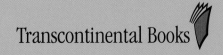

Transcontinental Books

WITH NEARLY 40 YEARS' WORTH OF RECIPES CREATED BY THE CANADIAN LIVING TEST KITCHEN, you can only imagine how many of them have been salads. But looking back at our "salad days" has made me realize that this dish has come a long way since the 1970s. The heyday of salads is now!

Our magazine has never been about serving a plate of iceberg lettuce and giant tomato wedges (drowned in Thousand Island dressing, of course!). But these days, with all the new, interesting and nutritious greens, grains, vegetables and fruit that are readily available in supermarkets, our options have become almost endless. In fact, we had so many great recipes in our repertoire that choosing just 150 was a bit of a challenge.

Whether you're looking for an elegant starter for a romantic dinner, a harvest medley for a holiday meal, an easy weeknight dinner salad, or a sweet and fruity dessert, we have just the recipe to fill the bill.

Eat well and enjoy!

Annabelle Waugh
director, Food

8 LEAFY & GREEN

HEARTY DINNER

60

112 BEAN & GRAIN

PASTA, POTATO & SLAW

164

Canadian Living

150 ESSENTIAL

SALADS

FRUIT & VEGETABLE

214

RECIPES

GRILLED PORTOBELLO SALAD
with arugula

A SHARP VEGETABLE PEELER SHAVES NEAT CURLS OFF THE SIDE OF A WEDGE OF PARMESAN CHEESE. IF YOU LIKE YOUR RED ONIONS A LITTLE MILDER, SOAK THE SLICES IN COLD WATER AND DRAIN BEFORE ADDING THEM TO THE SALAD.

INGREDIENTS

½ cup	walnut pieces
8	portobello mushrooms (about 450 g), stemmed and gills removed (see how-to, page 171)
10 cups	trimmed arugula (about 2 bunches)
Quarter	red onion, thinly sliced
60 g	Parmesan or Asiago cheese, shaved

Rosemary Balsamic Dressing:

½ cup	extra-virgin olive oil
¼ cup	balsamic vinegar
1 tbsp	chopped fresh rosemary or thyme (or 1 tsp dried)
¼ tsp	each salt and pepper

METHOD

In dry skillet, toast walnuts over medium heat, shaking pan occasionally, until golden, about 5 minutes. Set aside.

Rosemary Balsamic Dressing: Whisk together oil, vinegar, rosemary, salt and pepper; set aside.

Wipe tops of mushrooms with damp towel; cut in half. Brush with half of the dressing. Place on greased grill over medium-high heat; close lid and grill, turning once, until tender, about 10 minutes. (*Make-ahead: Let cool. Refrigerate in airtight container for up to 24 hours. Pour off any juices.*)

In large bowl, combine arugula, red onion and half of the walnuts. Add remaining dressing; toss to coat. Mound arugula mixture on platter; top with mushrooms. Sprinkle with Parmesan cheese and remaining walnuts.

TEST KITCHEN TIP These giant mushrooms vary in size; for this recipe, look for smaller ones that will give you eight to a pound (450 g). If you can't find them, use large portobellos and quarter them after grilling.

Makes 12 servings.

PER SERVING: about 158 cal, 5 g pro, 14 g total fat (2 g sat. fat), 6 g carb, 2 g fibre, 4 mg chol, 135 mg sodium. % RDI: 12% calcium, 8% iron, 12% vit A, 12% vit C, 25% folate.

BOSTON LETTUCE AND MÂCHE SALAD
with buttermilk dill dressing

THIS ELEGANT LITTLE SALAD IS AN IDEAL STARTER FOR ENTERTAINING. MAKE A BATCH OF THE CREAMY DRESSING WHENEVER YOU NEED TO USE UP BUTTERMILK THAT'S LEFT OVER FROM BAKING OR OTHER COOKING PROJECTS.

12

INGREDIENTS

2	small heads Boston lettuce
4 cups	mâche, baby spinach or trimmed arugula
4	radishes, thinly sliced
1	green onion, sliced

Buttermilk Dill Dressing:

⅔ cup	buttermilk
¼ cup	light mayonnaise
2 tbsp	minced fresh parsley
1 tsp	cider vinegar
½ tsp	Dijon mustard
¼ tsp	dried dillweed (see how-to, below)
Pinch	each salt and pepper

METHOD

Buttermilk Dill Dressing: Whisk together buttermilk, mayonnaise, parsley, vinegar, mustard, dill, salt and pepper. *(Make-ahead: Refrigerate in airtight container for up to 24 hours.)*

Cut each head of Boston lettuce into quarters. Keeping lettuce wedges intact, arrange mâche between leaves. Place each wedge on salad plate; sprinkle with radishes and green onion. Drizzle with dressing.

HOW TO
SUBSTITUTE FRESH HERBS FOR DRIED

Generally, you need three times as much of a fresh herb as you do of a dried herb to get the same intensity of flavour. So, for this recipe, you'd want to use about ¾ tsp chopped fresh dill in place of the dried. This guideline works for most recipes, but sometimes it pays to be a little cautious and start with slightly less, then add more to taste. You can always add, but you can't subtract.

Makes 8 servings.
PER SERVING: about 45 cal, 2 g pro, 3 g total fat (trace sat. fat), 4 g carb, I g fibre, 3 mg chol, 85 mg sodium. % RDI: 5% calcium, 6% iron, 25% vit A, 28% vit C, 18% folate.

GRILLED RADICCHIO SALAD

LETTUCE ISN'T OFTEN SEEN AS A GRILLING VEGETABLE, BUT RADICCHIO DEFIES THAT REPUTATION.
ITS NATURAL BITTER EDGE IS TEMPERED BY THE SMOKE AND SWEET CARAMELIZATION
THE BARBECUE ADDS. THIS RECIPE IS EASILY DOUBLED FOR A LARGER CROWD.

METHOD

Leaving cores intact, cut radicchio in half (cut large heads into quarters). Thread onto metal or soaked wooden skewers (see tip, page 180); brush with oil.

Place on greased grill over medium-high heat; close lid and grill, turning three times, until wilted and browned and centre is softened, about 8 minutes. Cut out cores; thinly slice radicchio. Set aside.

Sherry Mustard Vinaigrette: In large bowl, whisk together oil, vinegar, garlic, mustard, salt, pepper and sugar. Add radicchio; toss to coat. Sprinkle with Parmesan cheese.

INGREDIENTS

2	heads radicchio
4 tsp	vegetable oil
2 tbsp	shaved Parmesan cheese

Sherry Mustard Vinaigrette:

2 tbsp	extra-virgin olive oil
1 tbsp	sherry vinegar or wine vinegar
1	clove garlic, minced
½ tsp	Dijon mustard
Pinch	each salt and pepper
Pinch	granulated sugar

Makes 4 servings.
PER SERVING: about 135 cal, 3 g pro, 12 g total fat (2 g sat. fat), 4 g carb, 1 g fibre, 3 mg chol, 75 mg sodium. % RDI: 5% calcium, 4% iron, 1% vit A, 10% vit C, 17% folate.

SPICY GREENS
with maple soy vinaigrette

SLIGHTLY SPICY MIXED BITTER GREENS, SUCH AS MIZUNA, ARUGULA, ESCAROLE, FRISÉE AND WATERCRESS, MAKE AN IDEAL BACKDROP FOR THE VINAIGRETTE'S TOUCH OF MAPLE SWEETNESS. THE DRESSING IS GOOD WITH JUST ABOUT ANY COMBINATION OF MIXED GREENS, HOWEVER, SO USE WHATEVER YOU HAVE ON HAND.

METHOD

Maple Soy Vinaigrette: In large bowl, whisk together vegetable oil, vinegar, soy sauce, maple syrup and sesame oil.

Add mixed greens and carrot; toss to coat.

INGREDIENTS

8 cups	loosely packed mixed greens
1	carrot, grated

Maple Soy Vinaigrette:

2 tbsp	vegetable oil
1 tbsp	unseasoned rice vinegar
2 tsp	soy sauce
2 tsp	maple syrup (see how-to, below)
1 tsp	sesame oil

HOW TO
CHOOSE THE RIGHT MAPLE SYRUP

To ensure you're getting real maple syrup, check the label: It must bear the name, grade and colour class of syrup, and the name and address of the producer or packer. The Canadian Food Inspection Agency monitors the safety and quality of maple syrup, and classifies it into three grades, with five different colour classes. Canada No. 1 comes in three colour classes: Extra light and light are pale and mild flavoured; medium is also light in colour but has a rich maple flavour. Medium is the most popular choice for table syrup, and it's perfect for the maple dressing on this page. Canada No. 2 (amber) is usually made later in the sugaring season and has a dark, strong flavour that makes it great for cooking (though some prefer it as a rich table syrup). Canada No. 3 (dark) is made at the end of the season. It is very dark, with a strong, molasses-like flavour and is used commercially.

Makes 4 servings.
PER SERVING: about 107 cal, 2 g pro, 8 g total fat (1 g sat. fat), 8 g carb, 2 g fibre, 0 mg chol, 191 mg sodium, 400 mg potassium. % RDI: 7% calcium, 6% iron, 48% vit A, 27% vit C, 44% folate.

DANDELION SALAD
with warm bacon mushroom dressing

RICH BACON AND EGG YOLKS CUT THE NATURAL BITTERNESS OF DANDELION IN THIS FRENCH BISTRO CLASSIC.
THE GREENS ARE PACKED WITH VITAMINS AND MINERALS, SO THEY'RE A VERY NUTRITIOUS OPTION.

INGREDIENTS

4	slices bacon
1 tbsp	extra-virgin olive oil
2 cups	oyster mushrooms, sliced
1	shallot, thinly sliced
2 tbsp	red wine vinegar
1 tsp	Dijon mustard
¼ tsp	pepper
8 cups	dandelion greens, cut in 2-inch (5 cm) lengths
4	fried eggs (see how-to, below)

METHOD

In skillet, cook bacon over medium-high heat until crisp, about 6 minutes. Reserving 2 tbsp of the fat, drain bacon on paper towel–lined plate. Chop into bite-size pieces.

In same skillet, heat reserved bacon fat and oil over medium heat; cook mushrooms and shallot, stirring occasionally, until tender and golden, about 6 minutes. Remove from heat; let stand for 1 minute. Whisk in vinegar, mustard and pepper.

Place greens in large bowl; drizzle with mushroom mixture. Add bacon; toss to coat. Divide salad among four plates; top each with fried egg.

HOW TO

MAKE PERFECT FRIED EGGS

Fried eggs are a heavenly topping for many dishes, including stir-fries, fried rice and salads. Here's how to make them just the way you like them.

Sunny-side-up eggs: In large nonstick skillet, melt 2 tsp butter over medium heat. Crack 4 eggs into skillet; fry just until whites are set, about 3 minutes.

Over-easy eggs: Same as sunny-side-up, but fry until whites are set, then turn over and fry just until white film forms over yolks, about 30 seconds.

Makes 4 servings.
PER SERVING: about 277 cal, 13 g pro, 20 g total fat (6 g sat. fat), 13 g carb, 5 g fibre, 227 mg chol, 357 mg sodium. % RDI: 22% calcium, 36% iron, 164% vit A, 65% vit C, 28% folate.

Great Salad Greens

Salads can be as creative as you want them to be, thanks to the huge assortment of greens available. Here are some common varieties and less-familiar ones you can add to your rotation.

Mild Greens

BABY GREENS
A variety of greens from 4 to 6 inches (10 to 15 cm) long, ranging from mild-tasting lettuce to spicy mustard or beet greens. These make an attractive, delicate salad.

BUTTERHEAD LETTUCE
Soft, pale, buttery leaves with mild flavour, such as Boston and Bibb. Also called "butter lettuce," it's great for sandwiches and salads.

ICEBERG LETTUCE
Crisp, watery leaves with an extremely mild flavour. This is the lettuce for taco salad and other dishes that require a crunchy, unobtrusive type of green.

LEAF LETTUCE
Curly, delicate leaves with a very mild flavour. This lettuce comes in red and green varieties, which make beautiful salads.

MÂCHE
Small, tender leaves with a mild, nutty, sweet flavour, grown in low clumps rather than heads. Also known as lamb's lettuce or corn salad, mâche works well in the same types of salads that butterhead lettuce does.

ROMAINE LETTUCE
Long, sturdy and crisp pale green leaves with a classic lettuce flavour. It's a must-have for Caesar salad.

SPINACH
Firm, dark green leaves with an earthy but mild flavour. Spinach is ideal in salads, cooked into pastas and pastries, or served as a sautéed vegetable. Baby spinach has a more delicate texture and doesn't require stemming.

Spicy or Bitter Greens

ARUGULA
Soft, dark green pepper-flavoured leaves. Arugula is wonderful in salads and pastas, and on pizzas. Baby arugula has tender stems that don't need to be trimmed.

BELGIAN ENDIVE
Long white to pale yellow-green leaves grown in tight, elongated heads, with a bitter flavour and a crunchy texture. Not to be confused with curly endive, Belgian endive is excellent filled as an hors d'oeuvre and is also tasty in mixed greens salads.

ESCAROLE
Deep green, sturdy leaves in a compact head, with a bitter flavour. Young leaves are nice in salads, while more mature ones are better wilted in soups or served as a side dish.

FRISÉE
Crisp curly-edged leaves that go from deep green outside to pale inside, with a bitter taste. Also known as curly chicory or curly endive, it's excellent in mixed greens salads.

MIZUNA
Tender, elongated, spiky green leaves, with a refreshing, peppery flavour. Try mizuna in any dish where you would use arugula.

RADICCHIO
Gorgeous deep purple-red leaves with white veins, with a pleasantly bitter flavour. Radicchio is one of the few lettuces you'll see cooked, and it's fabulous grilled. It's also a staple in mixed greens salads, and pairs very well with romaine lettuce.

ASPARAGUS AND MIXED GREENS SALAD

ASPARAGUS IS ONE OF THE DARLINGS OF SPRING, AND THIS SALAD SHOWS IT OFF GLORIOUSLY. FENNEL SEEDS GIVE THE VINAIGRETTE A PLEASANT HINT OF LICORICE FLAVOUR THAT COMPLEMENTS THE EARTHY GREENS; PRESS THEM LIGHTLY WITH A HEAVY SAUCEPAN TO CRUSH AND RELEASE THEIR AROMA.

METHOD

Bake pecans on rimmed baking sheet in 350°F (180°C) oven until lightly toasted, about 8 minutes. Let cool. *(Make-ahead: Store in airtight container for up to 5 days.)*

Lemon Fennel Vinaigrette: Meanwhile, whisk together oil, shallot, lemon juice, mustard, honey, fennel seeds, salt and pepper. Set aside. *(Make-ahead: Refrigerate in airtight container for up to 3 days. Shake or whisk to combine.)*

Toss together asparagus, oil, salt and pepper. Bake on rimmed baking sheet in 350°F (180°C) oven until tender-crisp, 6 to 8 minutes. Let cool; cover and refrigerate. *(Make-ahead: Refrigerate in airtight container for up to 24 hours.)*

Arrange asparagus on salad plates. In large bowl, toss together pecans, frisée, arugula, watercress, Boston lettuce and vinaigrette; divide over asparagus. Serve immediately.

INGREDIENTS

1 cup	pecan pieces
1	bunch (450 g) asparagus, trimmed (see how-to, page 175)
2 tsp	olive oil
Pinch	each salt and pepper
4 cups	torn frisée
4 cups	baby arugula
4 cups	trimmed watercress
1	head Boston lettuce, torn

Lemon Fennel Vinaigrette:

¼ cup	olive oil
3 tbsp	minced shallot
3 tbsp	lemon juice
2 tsp	Dijon mustard
2 tsp	liquid honey
1½ tsp	crushed fennel seeds
½ tsp	each salt and pepper

Makes 8 servings.

PER SERVING: about 200 cal, 4 g pro, 18 g total fat (2 g sat. fat), 9 g carb, 4 g fibre, 0 mg chol, 188 mg sodium, 458 mg potassium. % RDI: 10% calcium, 13% iron, 28% vit A, 32% vit C, 65% folate.

HARVEST SALAD

AT A GLANCE, THIS MAY LOOK LIKE AN EVERYTHING-BUT-THE-KITCHEN-SINK SALAD,
BUT ITS SEASONAL INGREDIENTS MELD BEAUTIFULLY. SOAKING THE SHALLOTS IN VINEGAR
PICKLES THEM SLIGHTLY, GIVING THE SALAD A TANGY ACCENT.

INGREDIENTS

3 cups	cubed pumpernickel or rye bread
1	pkg (115 g) mâche or mixed baby greens
3	heads Belgian endive, separated into leaves
115 g	blue cheese, crumbled
2	hard-cooked eggs (see how-to, page 79), quartered
1	apple, cored and cut in chunks
½ cup	walnut halves

Caraway Dressing:

2 tsp	caraway seeds
⅓ cup	finely chopped shallots or onion
3 tbsp	white wine vinegar
¼ tsp	salt
1 tbsp	Dijon mustard
1	clove garlic, minced
¼ tsp	white pepper
⅓ cup	extra-virgin olive oil

METHOD

Bake bread cubes on rimmed baking sheet in 350°F (180°C) oven until crisp, about 10 minutes. Transfer to large bowl.

Caraway Dressing: Meanwhile, in small dry skillet, toast caraway seeds over medium-low heat until fragrant, about 2 minutes. Let cool slightly. In mortar with pestle or using bottom of heavy pot, crush caraway seeds.

In small bowl, combine shallots, vinegar and salt; let stand for 5 minutes. Stir in mustard, garlic, pepper and caraway seeds; whisk in oil.

To bowl with croutons, add mâche, Belgian endive, blue cheese, eggs, apple and walnuts. Pour dressing over top; toss to coat.

HOW TO

STORE DRIED HERBS AND SPICES

Dried herbs and spices are a must-have in your pantry. They may seem to keep indefinitely, but their flavours do diminish over time. For best results, buy them in small amounts, and store them in airtight containers for no longer than six months. A cool, dark place, such as a cupboard (ideally, away from the dishwasher, sink and stove), will protect them from heat, humidity and light, all of which can weaken their potency. Discard any old herbs and spices regularly, and rotate in a fresh supply to give your recipes the best flavour.

Makes 8 servings.

PER SERVING: about 246 cal, 8 g pro, 19 g total fat (5 g sat. fat), 13 g carb, 3 g fibre, 57 mg chol, 399 mg sodium, 268 mg potassium. % RDI: 11% calcium, 10% iron, 16% vit A, 13% vit C, 17% folate.

GREEK-STYLE ROMAINE SALAD

TRADITIONAL GREEK VILLAGE SALAD CONTAINS NO GREENS, BUT MOST GREEK RESTAURANTS IN NORTH AMERICA INCLUDE LETTUCE. HERE, STURDY ROMAINE TAKES THE PLACE OF SOFTER ICEBERG AND GIVES THE SALAD A LITTLE MORE OOMPH.

INGREDIENTS

4 cups	torn romaine lettuce
1 cup	cherry tomatoes, quartered
1 cup	cubed English cucumber
Half	sweet green pepper, chopped
⅓ cup	sliced red onion
¼ cup	crumbled feta cheese
8	Kalamata olives

Garlic and Oregano Dressing:

2 tbsp	extra-virgin olive oil
1 tbsp	red wine vinegar
1	small clove garlic, minced
¼ tsp	dried oregano
Pinch	pepper

METHOD

Garlic and Oregano Dressing: In glass measure, whisk together oil, vinegar, garlic, oregano and pepper; set aside.

In large bowl, toss together lettuce, tomatoes, cucumber, green pepper and red onion. Drizzle dressing over top; toss to coat. Sprinkle with feta cheese and olives.

Makes 4 to 6 servings.

PER EACH OF 6 SERVINGS: about 86 cal, 2 g pro, 7 g total fat (2 g sat. fat), 5 g carb, 2 g fibre, 6 mg chol, 180 mg sodium. % RDI: 5% calcium, 5% iron, 22% vit A, 32% vit C, 24% folate.

Washing and Storing Salad Greens

A thorough washing will ensure your fresh greens remain top-quality and grit-free.
Here's how to do it easily, plus what you need to know to keep your greens fresh for days.

1. Place the greens in a bowl or clean sink filled with cold water. (Avoid running water over greens, because it can bruise and damage delicate leaves.)

2. Gently swish the greens around with your hands to remove any fine grit. Lift the greens into a salad spinner instead of pouring or draining so that the grit doesn't resettle into the leaf folds.

3. Spin the greens for a few seconds, draining between rotations. If the water still looks gritty, repeat the process. No salad spinner? Lay the "lifted" greens on a clean tea towel or pillowcase. Gather the edges together to make a bundle and shake gently.

4. Lay the spun greens on a clean tea towel or paper towels. Very loosely roll up the towel with the greens inside, and store it in an unsealed plastic bag in the crisper drawer of the refrigerator. Your greens should keep for up to a week.

Get Your 10 a Day

It's surprisingly easy to increase your daily intake of vegetables and fruits.
Here are some simple ways to get the recommended seven to 10 servings per day.

BREAKFAST
- Add veggies to an omelette or scrambled eggs.
- Start with a smoothie, combining up to three different fruits or veggies.
- Layer dried or fresh fruits with yogurt and granola.

LUNCH
- Use mashed avocado instead of mayonnaise on sandwiches.
- Add vegetables to sandwiches. In addition to lettuce and tomato, consider sliced sweet peppers, grated carrots and sprouts.
- To help curb sweet cravings later on, have some fresh fruit after lunch.

DINNER
- Immediately after purchasing it, wash, prep and package produce. Prepped veggies are more likely to be added to last-minute meals.
- Garnish food with fruits or veggies, such as apple on curry or fresh tomato salsa on grilled chicken.
- Add extra vegetables to everyday meals, such as grated carrot and zucchini to pasta sauce, meat loaf or chili, or roasted veggies to rice or pasta dishes.

SNACKS
- Keep a selection of fruits on the counter. The more you see them, the more you'll want one.
- Prepare vegetable crudités to store in the fridge. When they're ready, you'll munch on them easily.
- Craving something sweet? Opt for dried fruit mixes instead of baked goods or chocolate.

MIXED GREENS
with orange chive dressing

A SUNNY ORANGE-STUDDED SALAD IS JUST THE THING FOR A SUMMER BARBECUE, BUT IT WORKS
EQUALLY WELL TO DRIVE AWAY THE CHILL OF A WINTER EVENING. INSTEAD OF PACKAGED SALAD GREENS,
YOU CAN EASILY MAKE YOUR OWN MIX OF MÂCHE (OR BABY SPINACH), FRISÉE, BOSTON LETTUCE AND ARUGULA.

METHOD

Orange Chive Dressing: Working over bowl, cut off rind and outer membrane of oranges; cut between membrane and pulp to release sections into bowl. Spoon 2 tbsp of the orange juice into separate bowl; save remainder for another use. Whisk in oil, chives, mustard, salt and pepper; set dressing aside.

With sharp chef's knife or mandoline, thinly slice fennel lengthwise. Place in large bowl; toss with 2 tbsp of the dressing.

Add mixed greens, orange sections and remaining dressing; toss to coat.

INGREDIENTS

Half	bulb fennel, cored
5 cups	torn mixed greens

Orange Chive Dressing:

3	oranges
3 tbsp	vegetable oil
1 tbsp	chopped fresh chives
½ tsp	Dijon mustard
¼ tsp	each salt and pepper

Makes 6 servings.
PER SERVING: about 97 cal, 2 g pro, 7 g total fat (1 g sat. fat), 9 g carb, 2 g fibre, 0 mg chol,
122 mg sodium, 308 mg potassium. % RDI: 5% calcium, 4% iron, 11% vit A, 58% vit C, 27% folate.

KOHLRABI, RED APPLE AND WALNUT SALAD

KOHLRABI LOOKS A LITTLE LIKE A TINY ALIEN'S HEAD, BUT DON'T LET THAT DISSUADE YOU FROM PICKING IT UP FOR THIS SALAD. ITS DELICATE BROCCOLI-STEM FLAVOUR WORKS SO WELL WITH THIS JAZZY MIX OF SWEET APPLE, CREAMY BLUE CHEESE AND WALNUTS.

INGREDIENTS

½ cup	walnut pieces
85 g	blue cheese, crumbled
⅓ cup	0% plain Greek yogurt
2 tbsp	lemon juice
1 tbsp	milk
2 tbsp	thinly sliced fresh chives
Dash	hot pepper sauce
Pinch	each salt and pepper
1	red-skinned apple
2	kohlrabi, trimmed, peeled, halved and thinly sliced in half-moons
6 cups	baby arugula

METHOD

Toast walnuts on rimmed baking sheet in 350°F (180°C) oven until light golden, 6 to 8 minutes. Let cool.

Set aside 2 tbsp of the blue cheese for garnish. In bowl, combine remaining blue cheese, yogurt, 1 tbsp of the lemon juice and milk, mashing with fork until almost smooth. Stir in chives, hot pepper sauce, salt and pepper; set dressing aside.

Cut apple in half; core and thinly slice. In large bowl, toss apple with remaining lemon juice. Add kohlrabi and arugula; toss with dressing to coat. Garnish with walnuts and reserved blue cheese.

Makes 6 servings.

PER SERVING: about 150 cal, 7 g pro, 11 g total fat (3 g sat. fat), 9 g carb, 3 g fibre, 12 mg chol, 218 mg sodium, 283 mg potassium. % RDI: 15% calcium, 6% iron, 9% vit A, 38% vit C, 19% folate.

BORGONZOLA AND WALNUT SALAD

BLUE CHEESE AND WALNUTS ARE A MATCH MADE IN HEAVEN, ESPECIALLY WHEN THEY'RE PARTNERED WITH A CRISP SALAD. CALIFORNIA WALNUT HALVES ARE THE FRESHEST, BUT ARE PRICEY AND CAN GO RANCID QUICKLY. STOCK UP WHEN THEY'RE ON SALE, THEN FREEZE THEM IN RESEALABLE BAGS SO YOU CAN USE JUST WHAT YOU NEED LATER ON.

INGREDIENTS

¾ cup	walnut halves
¼ cup	extra-virgin olive oil
2 tbsp	minced red onion
4 tsp	balsamic vinegar
1 tbsp	red wine vinegar
2	anchovy fillets, minced (or 1 tsp anchovy paste), see tip, page 37
1	small clove garlic, minced
¼ tsp	pepper
Pinch	salt
1	small head radicchio, torn or cut in pieces
1	head Boston lettuce, torn or cut in pieces
1	bunch arugula, trimmed
175 g	Borgonzola cheese, cut or broken in chunks

METHOD

In dry skillet over medium heat, toast walnuts until fragrant, about 4 minutes. Let cool.

In large bowl, whisk together oil, red onion, balsamic vinegar, wine vinegar, anchovies, garlic, pepper and salt. Add radicchio, Boston lettuce and arugula; toss to coat. Top with Borgonzola cheese and walnuts.

TEST KITCHEN TIP

Borgonzola is a Canadian hybrid of Brie and Gorgonzola cheeses; it has a creamy, mild Brie flavour with a sharp blue tang. If you can't find it or want a slightly fancier salad, Italian Gorgonzola is a wonderful (but pricier) alternative.

Makes 6 to 8 servings.

PER EACH OF 8 SERVINGS: about 212 cal, 8 g pro, 22 g total fat (7 g sat. fat), 5 g carb, 1 g fibre, 30 mg chol, 181 mg sodium, 254 mg potassium. % RDI: 9% calcium, 6% iron, 7% vit A, 10% vit C, 24% folate.

WARM PEAR AND HAZELNUT SALAD

LIKE BORGONZOLA CHEESE (SEE TIP, OPPOSITE), CAMBOZOLA IS A HYBRID, WITH A FLAVOUR REMINISCENT OF BOTH CAMEMBERT AND GORGONZOLA. RIPE PEARS ARE THE IDEAL COMPLEMENT; MAKE SURE THEY'RE FRAGRANT BUT STILL FIRM TO THE TOUCH FOR THE BEST TEXTURE. THIS SALAD SERVES FOUR AS A MAIN DISH OR EIGHT AS A STARTER.

29

METHOD

In skillet, melt butter over medium-high heat; cook pears for 1 minute. Add 1 tbsp of the vinegar and brown sugar; toss to coat. Cook until fork-tender, about 2 minutes.

Meanwhile, in large bowl, whisk together remaining vinegar, olive oil, mustard, honey, salt and pepper. Toss with arugula. Divide among four plates; sprinkle with Cambozola cheese, hazelnuts and warm pears.

CHANGE IT UP

WARM APPLE AND HAZELNUT SALAD

Substitute the same amount of baby spinach for the arugula and tart apples for the pears.

INGREDIENTS

1 tbsp	butter
2	firm ripe pears (such as Bartlett), cored and cut in ¼-inch (5 mm) thick slices
3 tbsp	sherry vinegar
1 tbsp	packed brown sugar
3 tbsp	olive oil
1 tsp	Dijon mustard
1 tsp	liquid honey
¼ tsp	each salt and pepper
12 cups	baby arugula
100 g	Cambozola cheese, broken in chunks
¼ cup	skinned toasted hazelnuts (see how-to, below)

HOW TO

TOAST AND SKIN HAZELNUTS

Toast the nuts in a single layer on rimmed baking sheet in 350°F (180°C) oven until fragrant and skins crack, about 10 minutes. Let cool slightly, then transfer nuts to tea towel. Briskly rub towel over nuts to remove as much of the skin as possible. Pick skinned nuts off towel, and they're ready to use.

Makes 4 servings.

PER SERVING: about 365 cal, 7 g pro, 29 g total fat (10 g sat. fat), 22 g carb, 5 g fibre, 37 mg chol, 551 mg sodium, 416 mg potassium. % RDI: 23% calcium, 12% iron, 27% vit A, 20% vit C, 35% folate.

ENDIVE SALAD
with herbed goat cheese

HERB-COATED GOAT CHEESE SPREAD OVER CROÛTES IS FAR TASTIER THAN JUST PLAIN CROUTONS.
PREP THE CHEESE, WASH THE GREENS AND BAKE THE CROÛTES AHEAD SO THE ASSEMBLY TAKES JUST MINUTES.

METHOD

Croûtes: Cut baguette into twelve ½-inch (1 cm) thick slices; rub one side of each with cut side of garlic. Brush with oil; sprinkle with salt and pepper. Bake on rimmed baking sheet in 350°F (180°C) oven until crisp and light golden, about 8 minutes. Let cool. *(Make-ahead: Store in airtight container for up to 24 hours.)*

Lemon Vinaigrette: Whisk together oil, lemon juice, mustard, sugar, salt and pepper. *(Make-ahead: Cover and refrigerate for up to 24 hours.)*

On waxed paper, combine chives, parsley and herbes de Provence; roll goat cheese in herb mixture to coat. *(Make-ahead: Wrap in plastic wrap and refrigerate for up to 24 hours.)*

Toss mixed greens with vinaigrette; arrange on six plates. Top each salad with three Belgian endive leaves. Cut goat cheese into six slices; place one slice on each salad. Add two croûtes to each plate.

INGREDIENTS

2 tbsp	each chopped fresh chives and parsley
½ tsp	herbes de Provence or dried thyme
1	log (113 g) soft goat cheese
6 cups	torn mixed greens
18	leaves Belgian endive (about 1 large head)

Lemon Vinaigrette:

3 tbsp	vegetable oil
2 tsp	lemon juice
½ tsp	Dijon mustard
¼ tsp	granulated sugar
Pinch	each salt and pepper

Croûtes:

1	baguette
Half	clove garlic
2 tsp	extra-virgin olive oil
¼ tsp	sea salt or salt
¼ tsp	pepper

Makes 6 servings.

PER SERVING: about 292 cal, 9 g pro, 17 g total fat (4 g sat. fat), 27 g carb, 3 g fibre, 9 mg chol, 438 mg sodium. % RDI: 10% calcium, 16% iron, 19% vit A, 18% vit C, 41% folate.

MIXED GREENS
with chive vinaigrette

RADISHES ARE ONE OF THE FIRST (AND QUICKEST) VEGETABLES TO POP UP IN THE GARDEN. THIS SALAD IS A PERFECTLY DELICIOUS WAY TO USE UP THESE TENDER VEGGIES WHEN THEY ARE AT THEIR PEAK FLAVOUR.

32

INGREDIENTS

8 cups	torn mixed greens
1 cup	thinly sliced radishes

Chive Vinaigrette:

¼ cup	vegetable oil
2 tbsp	chopped fresh chives or green onions
2 tbsp	white wine vinegar
½ tsp	Dijon mustard
¼ tsp	each salt and pepper
¼ tsp	dried tarragon or thyme

METHOD

Chive Vinaigrette: Whisk together oil, chives, vinegar, mustard, salt, pepper and tarragon. *(Make-ahead: Cover and set aside for up to 2 hours; whisk to combine.)*

In large bowl, toss mixed greens with radishes. Pour vinaigrette over top; toss to coat.

Wine vinegars are less boldly acidic than white or cider vinegars and make good bases for salad dressings. White wine vinegar is milder than red wine vinegar, so it's perfect for delicate sauces and dressings like the vinaigrette on this page. If you don't have any on hand, you can try red wine vinegar, but it will give the dressing a stronger flavour and a pinkish hue. Champagne vinegar and unseasoned rice vinegar are better substitutes.

Makes 8 servings.
PER SERVING: about 74 cal, I g pro, 7 g total fat (I g sat. fat), 2 g carb, I g fibre, 0 mg chol, 93 mg sodium. % RDI: 4% calcium, 4% iron, 12% vit A, 18% vit C, 23% folate.

ENDIVE AND APPLE SALAD
with fried camembert

THIS DISH IS AN ELEGANT FIRST COURSE FOR SIX OR MAIN COURSE FOR FOUR. IF YOU WANT TO PAIR WINE WITH IT, TRY A HERBACEOUS SAUVIGNON BLANC, A CRISP UNOAKED CANADIAN CHARDONNAY OR A FRENCH CHABLIS.

METHOD

Cider Dijon Vinaigrette: In small bowl, whisk together vinegar, mustard, salt and pepper; whisk in vegetable and olive oils.

In large bowl, combine Belgian endive, mâche, apple and onion. Set salad and vinaigrette aside.

Cut cheese into four to six wedges. Place flour, egg and bread crumbs in separate shallow bowls. Coat each cheese wedge in flour, gently shaking off excess; dip in egg, letting excess drip back into dish. Dip again in flour, then in egg. Coat with bread crumbs, pressing to cover completely.

In skillet, pour in enough oil to come ½ inch (1 cm) up side; heat over medium-high heat. Fry cheese, turning once, until golden, 1 to 2 minutes per side. Drain on paper towel–lined plate.

Toss Belgian endive mixture with vinaigrette; divide among plates. Top each with cheese wedge.

INGREDIENTS

4 cups	chopped Belgian endive
4 cups	mâche or trimmed watercress
1	red-skinned apple, quartered, cored and thinly sliced
½ cup	thinly sliced sweet onion
1	round (about 370 g) Camembert cheese
¼ cup	all-purpose flour
1	egg, beaten
1¼ cups	fine fresh bread crumbs
	Vegetable oil for frying

Cider Dijon Vinaigrette:

2 tbsp	cider vinegar
2 tsp	Dijon mustard
Pinch	each salt and pepper
2 tbsp	vegetable oil
2 tbsp	extra-virgin olive oil

PHOTO
PAGE 34

Makes 4 to 6 servings.

PER EACH OF 6 SERVINGS: about 380 cal, 16 g pro, 29 g total fat (11 g sat. fat), 16 g carb, 3 g fibre, 75 mg chol, 609 mg sodium, 390 mg potassium. % RDI: 27% calcium, 8% iron, 28% vit A, 22% vit C, 40% folate.

ENDIVE AND APPLE SALAD
with fried camembert

PAGE 33

CABBAGE AND CAULIFLOWER SALAD

FOR A BOOST OF BETA-CAROTENE, LOOK FOR ORANGE CAULIFLOWER, WHICH HAS ABOUT 25 TIMES MORE BETA-CAROTENE THAN WHITE CAULIFLOWER DOES. YOU'LL FIND JICAMA IN THE PRODUCE SECTION; IT LOOKS LIKE A LARGE, SQUAT, KNOBBY ROOT VEGETABLE WITH ROUGH BROWN SKIN.

36

INGREDIENTS

6 cups	mixed baby greens
2½ cups	cooked cauliflower florets
1 cup	shredded red cabbage
1 cup	cubed old Cheddar cheese
½ cup	julienned jicama (see how-to, below)
½ cup	thinly sliced fennel bulb
1 cup	small Granny Smith apple, cored and sliced

Parsley Lemon Dressing:

2 tbsp	chopped fresh parsley
2 tbsp	extra-virgin olive oil
2 tbsp	canola oil
1 tsp	grated lemon zest
2 tbsp	lemon juice
1 tbsp	minced shallot
1	small clove garlic, minced
Pinch	each salt and pepper

METHOD

Parsley Lemon Dressing: Whisk together parsley, olive oil, canola oil, lemon zest, lemon juice, shallot, garlic, salt and pepper; set aside.

In large bowl, toss together baby greens, cauliflower, cabbage, Cheddar cheese, jicama, fennel and apple. Add dressing; toss to coat.

HOW TO

JULIENNE VEGETABLES QUICKLY

You can julienne vegetables by hand, but it is tedious. Speed things up by using a mandoline fitted with a julienne blade. Just use the hand guard and watch your fingers carefully, as the blades are incredibly sharp.

Makes 4 servings.

PER SERVING: about 319 cal, 12 g pro, 25 g total fat (8 g sat. fat), 15 g carb, 5 g fibre, 35 mg chol, 247 mg sodium. % RDI: 30% calcium, 11% iron, 29% vit A, 115% vit C, 56% folate.

BOSTON LETTUCE SALAD
with green goddess dressing

GREEN GODDESS DRESSING IS ONE OF THOSE VINTAGE RECIPES THAT NEVER SEEMS TO GO OUT OF STYLE.
FOR A LOWER-CALORIE TAKE ON IT, USE LIGHT MAYONNAISE AND SOUR CREAM.

METHOD

Green Goddess Dressing: If using anchovy fillet, soak in cold water for 5 minutes; drain, pat dry and chop.

In food processor, pulse together parsley, sour cream, mayonnaise, chives, vinegar, tarragon, salt, pepper, and anchovy (if using); whirl until smooth. *(Make-ahead: Refrigerate in airtight container for up to 24 hours.)*

In large bowl, toss together lettuce, arugula and radishes. Divide among salad bowls or plates; spoon dressing over top.

INGREDIENTS

6 cups	torn Boston or Bibb lettuce
2 cups	baby arugula or baby spinach
4	radishes, thinly sliced

Green Goddess Dressing:

1	anchovy fillet (or 1 tsp anchovy paste), optional (see tip, below)
1 cup	chopped fresh parsley
½ cup	sour cream
½ cup	mayonnaise
2 tbsp	thinly sliced fresh chives or green onions
2 tbsp	white wine vinegar
1 tbsp	dried tarragon (see how-to, page 12)
¼ tsp	each salt and pepper

TEST KITCHEN TIP

Recipes often call for only a few anchovy fillets, leaving you with extras. To store them, wrap the open can tightly in plastic wrap and refrigerate. (Better yet, look for resealable glass jars of anchovy fillets.) Unopened cans and jars will keep for about a year in the pantry; opened, they'll last for a couple of months in the fridge. Anchovy paste is a handy substitute for anchovy fillets. It has a milder flavour, but it comes in a resealable tube that lets you dispense just the amount you need. Look for it near the canned fish in the grocery store.

Makes 8 servings.
PER SERVING: about 135 cal, 2 g pro, 13 g total fat (3 g sat. fat), 3 g carb, 1 g fibre, 11 mg chol, 168 mg sodium. % RDI: 6% calcium, 7% iron, 17% vit A, 28% vit C, 27% folate.

POMEGRANATE CLEMENTINE FRISÉE SALAD

THE JUICY FLESH SURROUNDING POMEGRANATE SEEDS HAS JUST THE RIGHT
SWEET-TART BALANCE TO COMPLEMENT THE CLEMENTINES AND THE BITTER-EDGED FRISÉE IN
THIS SALAD. IT'S A FRESH, INVITING SIDE DISH FOR GRILLED MEATS OR FISH.

METHOD

In small dry skillet, toast walnuts over medium heat, turning occasionally, until lightly toasted, about 4 minutes; set aside.

Peel two of the clementines; divide fruit into sections. Using paring knife, remove as much white pith as possible from sections. Juice remaining clementines; set aside.

In large bowl, whisk together oil, vinegar, clementine juice, sugar, salt and pepper. Add frisée, Boston lettuce, onion and clementine sections; toss to coat. Divide among salad plates. Sprinkle with pomegranate seeds and walnuts.

INGREDIENTS

3 tbsp	walnut halves
4	clementines
3 tbsp	extra-virgin olive oil
2 tbsp	red wine vinegar
Pinch	granulated sugar
Pinch	each salt and pepper
4 cups	coarsely chopped frisée
2 cups	torn Boston lettuce
Quarter	sweet onion, sliced in rings
½ cup	pomegranate seeds (see how-to, below)

HOW TO

EASILY REMOVE POMEGRANATE SEEDS

First, quarter the pomegranate. Fill a large bowl with cold water; using your hands, submerge each pomegranate quarter and pry it open to remove the seeds and separate them from the membrane. Using a slotted spoon (or your hands), remove the pieces of membrane and skin that have floated to the top of the water; discard. Drain the pomegranate seeds; pat dry.

Makes 4 servings.

PER SERVING: about 183 cal, 3 g pro, 14 g total fat (2 g sat. fat), 15 g carb, 2 g fibre, 0 mg chol, 16 mg sodium, 446 mg potassium. % RDI: 5% calcium, 7% iron, 13% vit A, 63% vit C, 54% folate.

SMOKY GREEN SALAD
with creamy almond dressing

FOR THIS GORGEOUS SALAD, TOAST THE PEPITAS IN A DRY SKILLET OVER MEDIUM HEAT UNTIL THEY TURN GOLDEN. IF YOU DON'T HAVE PEPITAS, SUBSTITUTE YOUR FAVOURITE KIND OF NUT OR SEED AS A GARNISH.

INGREDIENTS

4	slices double-smoked bacon or regular bacon
1	head red leaf lettuce, torn
6 cups	lightly packed trimmed spinach
115 g	smoked Gouda cheese, cubed
2 cups	thinly sliced cremini mushrooms
3 tbsp	toasted pepitas (see tip, page 218)

Creamy Almond Dressing:

3 tbsp	almond butter
2 tbsp	sherry vinegar or red wine vinegar
2 tbsp	light-tasting olive oil or vegetable oil
1 tbsp	liquid honey
¼ tsp	each smoked paprika and pepper
Pinch	salt

METHOD

In skillet, cook bacon over medium heat, turning once, until crisp, 5 to 8 minutes. Drain on paper towel–lined plate.

In large bowl, combine lettuce, spinach, Gouda cheese, mushrooms and pepitas.

Creamy Almond Dressing: Whisk together almond butter, vinegar, oil, 2 tbsp water, honey, paprika, pepper and salt until smooth.

Pour dressing over salad; toss to coat. Crumble bacon over top.

Double-smoked bacon is cured, unlike regular bacon, which is brined. Then it's smoked for more than twice as long as regular bacon, giving it a rich, intensely smoky flavour. It's also often cut into thicker slices, meaning each piece has a heftier chew that's really appealing. European-style butchers usually carry double-smoked bacon, but more and more supermarkets are offering mass-market versions.

Makes 8 servings.
PER SERVING: about 176 cal, 8 g pro, 14 g total fat (4 g sat. fat), 7 g carb, 1 g fibre, 20 mg chol, 219 mg sodium, 387 mg potassium. % RDI: 14% calcium, 14% iron, 53% vit A, 13% vit C, 31% folate.

PEA, FENNEL AND GOAT CHEESE SALAD

THIS SIMPLE—AND SIMPLY SCRUMPTIOUS—SALAD MAKES GREAT USE OF FRESH PEAS AND BABY GREENS. FEEL FREE TO SWAP OUT THE BABY SPINACH IN FAVOUR OF WHATEVER GREENS YOU LOVE OR CAN FIND AT THE MARKET. OUT OF SEASON, USE FROZEN PEAS IN PLACE OF THE FRESH.

METHOD

In saucepan of boiling salted water, cook peas until tender-crisp, about 2 minutes. Drain and pat dry; set aside.

Dressing: In large bowl, whisk together oil, lemon juice, salt, pepper and sugar.

Add spinach, fennel and peas; gently toss to coat. Sprinkle with goat cheese.

INGREDIENTS

1½ cups	shelled fresh peas
6 cups	lightly packed baby spinach
1	bulb fennel, cored and thinly sliced
⅓ cup	crumbled soft goat cheese

Dressing:

2 tbsp	extra-virgin olive oil
1 tbsp	lemon juice
Pinch	each salt and pepper
Pinch	granulated sugar

Makes 4 servings.

PER SERVING: about 166 cal, 7 g pro, 10 g total fat (3 g sat. fat), 14 g carb, 6 g fibre, 6 mg chol, 238 mg sodium, 642 mg potassium. % RDI: 10% calcium, 19% iron, 51% vit A, 46% vit C, 63% folate.

MANDARIN SPINACH SALAD

THIS RESTAURANT CLASSIC NEVER SEEMS TO LOSE ITS POPULARITY. IF YOU ADD THE OPTIONAL ALMONDS, GIVE THEM A QUICK TOAST (SEE TIP, BELOW) BEFORE YOU ADD THEM TO BOOST THEIR FLAVOUR AND MAKE THEM EXTRA CRUNCHY.

44

INGREDIENTS

2 tbsp	vegetable oil
1 tbsp	unseasoned rice vinegar
1 tsp	grainy mustard
Pinch	each salt and pepper
4 cups	baby spinach
½ cup	bean sprouts
¼ cup	sliced almonds (optional)
3	radishes, thinly sliced
1	green onion, sliced
1	can (284 mL) mandarin oranges, drained and patted dry

METHOD

In large bowl, whisk together oil, vinegar, grainy mustard, salt and pepper.

Add spinach, bean sprouts, almonds (if using), radishes, green onion and mandarin oranges; toss to coat.

Sliced and slivered almonds are very thin. Watch them carefully as they toast, because they can burn quickly. Toasting them in a dry skillet over medium-high heat on the stove is the easiest way to keep an eye on them. Shake the pan constantly, and take the nuts off the heat immediately when they're golden and fragrant. Transfer them to a bowl so they don't cook further.

Makes 4 servings.

PER SERVING: about 93 cal, 2 g pro, 7 g total fat (1 g sat. fat), 7 g carb, 2 g fibre, 0 mg chol, 43 mg sodium. % RDI: 4% calcium, 9% iron, 35% vit A, 47% vit C, 33% folate.

BITTER GREENS SALAD

THIS SIMPLY DRESSED SALAD IS AN EXCELLENT SHOWCASE FOR LOCALLY GROWN GREENS, WHICH YOU'LL FIND IN FARMER'S MARKETS EARLY IN THE SUMMER (SEE "GREAT SALAD GREENS," PAGE 17). PERUSE THE MARKET STALLS FOR YOUR FAVOURITES AND CHANGE THIS SALAD UP DEPENDING ON WHAT'S FRESHEST.

METHOD

In large bowl, toss together Boston lettuce, radicchio, Belgian endive, escarole and green onion.

Sprinkle lettuce mixture with oil, vinegar, salt and pepper; toss to coat.

INGREDIENTS

4 cups	torn Boston lettuce
4 cups	torn radicchio
2 cups	sliced Belgian endive
2 cups	torn escarole or frisée
1	green onion, sliced
⅓ cup	extra-virgin olive oil
¼ cup	wine vinegar, cider vinegar or fruit vinegar (see recipes, page 148)
¼ tsp	sea salt or salt
¼ tsp	pepper

TEST KITCHEN TIP

Farmer's markets are also terrific places to check out locally made fruit vinegars. Raspberry vinegar is an old-fashioned favourite that's excellent in salads, but other fruit vinegars, such as cranberry, blueberry and blackberry are wonderful, too. Explore interesting options made with plums, currants or citrus to make your salads sing.

Makes 6 to 8 servings.

PER EACH OF 8 SERVINGS: about 93 cal, 1 g pro, 9 g total fat (1 g sat. fat), 3 g carb, 1 g fibre, 0 mg chol, 58 mg sodium. % RDI: 2% calcium, 3% iron, 6% vit A, 10% vit C, 21% folate.

MARINATED KALE SALAD

KALE LEAVES ARE ON THE CHEWY SIDE, BUT WHEN THEY'RE CHOPPED AND MARINATED AS THEY ARE IN THIS RECIPE, THEY SOFTEN AND BECOME EASIER—AND MORE DELIGHTFUL—TO EAT. THIS SALAD IS A TASTY MÉLANGE OF SUPERFOODS: KALE, CHERRIES AND NUTS, ALL OF WHICH ARE PACKED WITH NUTRIENTS AND FLAVOUR.

INGREDIENTS

3 tbsp	olive oil
2 tbsp	orange juice
1 tbsp	liquid honey
1	bunch kale, stemmed and chopped (see how-to, below)
⅓ cup	dried cherries, chopped
⅓ cup	chopped hazelnuts, toasted

METHOD

In large bowl, whisk together oil, orange juice and honey; add kale and cherries. Toss to coat. Let stand for 1 hour.

Serve salad sprinkled with toasted hazelnuts.

HOW TO

STEM KALE LEAVES

Kale has thick, sturdy stems that run down the centres of the leaves. The stem is not as pleasant to eat as the leafy part, so it's usually removed. And it's easy: Place a kale leaf on a cutting board, and run the tip of a sharp chef's knife down either side of the stem. Lift out the stem. and use the remaining tender leaf in salads and side dishes.

Makes 6 to 8 servings.

PER EACH OF 8 SERVINGS: about 126 cal, 2 g pro, 8 g total fat, 1 g sat. fat, 13 g carb, 2 g fibre, 0 mg chol, 20 mg sodium, 251 mg potassium. % RDI: 7% calcium, 8% iron, 39% vit A, 88% vit C, 9% folate.

No-Fail Vinaigrettes

SUN-DRIED TOMATO VINAIGRETTE

This is a terrific dual-purpose dressing. Toss it with your favourite mix of salad greens or use it as a quick marinade for chicken.

¼ cup	drained oil-packed sun-dried tomatoes
2 tbsp	balsamic vinegar
1	clove garlic, minced
1 tsp	dried oregano
½ tsp	granulated sugar
¼ tsp	pepper
Pinch	salt (optional)
⅓ cup	extra-virgin olive oil

Rinse and pat sun-dried tomatoes dry; finely chop and place in small bowl. Whisk in ½ cup water, vinegar, garlic, oregano, sugar, pepper, and salt (if using). Whisking constantly, drizzle in oil in slow steady stream until combined. (*Make-ahead: Refrigerate in airtight container for up to 5 days.*)

Makes about 1 cup.
PER 1 TBSP: about 71 cal, trace pro, 5 g total fat (1 g sat. fat), 7 g carb, trace fibre, 0 mg chol, 5 mg sodium. % RDI: 1% iron, 3% vit C.

OREGANO RED WINE VINAIGRETTE

Simple and delightfully tangy, this easy vinaigrette is an essential recipe to have in your culinary repertoire. Use it on whatever greens you like.

⅓ cup	extra-virgin olive oil
⅓ cup	vegetable oil
3 tbsp	red wine vinegar
2 tsp	Dijon mustard
1	clove garlic, minced
1 tsp	dried oregano
½ tsp	each salt and pepper

In bowl, whisk together olive oil, vegetable oil, vinegar, 2 tbsp water, mustard, garlic, oregano, salt and pepper. (*Make-ahead: Refrigerate in airtight container for up to 5 days.*)

Makes about 1 cup.
PER 1 TBSP: about 81 cal, 0 g pro, 9 g total fat (1 g sat. fat), trace carb, 0 g fibre, 0 mg chol, 80 mg sodium. % RDI: 1% iron.

CRANBERRY SHALLOT VINAIGRETTE

This gorgeous red vinaigrette is perfectly seasonal on a winter holiday table, but it's convenient to make year-round thanks to frozen cranberry concentrate.

½ cup	frozen cranberry concentrate, thawed
¼ cup	vegetable oil
¼ cup	red wine vinegar
2 tsp	grainy mustard
2	shallots, minced
½ tsp	each salt and pepper

In bowl or jar, whisk or shake together cranberry concentrate, ¼ cup water, oil, vinegar, mustard, shallots, salt and pepper. (*Make-ahead: Refrigerate in airtight container for up to 5 days.*)

Makes about 1 cup.
PER 1 TBSP: about 51 cal, trace pro, 3 g total fat (trace sat. fat), 5 g carb, trace fibre, 0 mg chol, 81 mg sodium, 11 mg potassium. % RDI: 1% iron, 7% vit C.

TOSSED SALAD
with honey garlic dressing

ROASTING THE GARLIC MAKES THIS DRESSING CREAMY WITHOUT ACTUALLY ADDING ANY CREAM OR MAYO. THE GARLIC IS ALSO WONDERFUL IN ALL SORTS OF DISHES, SO ROAST AND FREEZE EXTRA FOR LATER.

METHOD

Honey Garlic Dressing: Trim top off garlic; wrap garlic in foil. Roast on baking sheet in 375°F (190°C) oven until very soft, about 35 minutes. Let cool.

Squeeze out garlic pulp into fine strainer; with back of spoon, press into bowl. Whisk in vinegar, honey, mustard, salt and pepper. Slowly whisk in olive and vegetable oils until emulsified. *(Make-ahead: Cover and refrigerate for up to 2 days. Let stand at room temperature for 20 minutes; whisk to blend, adding up to 2 tsp water, if desired, to thin.)*

In large bowl, toss together red and green lettuces, cabbage and dressing to coat. Sprinkle with radishes.

INGREDIENTS

5 cups	torn red leaf lettuce
5 cups	torn green leaf lettuce
1 cup	shredded red cabbage
¼ cup	sliced radishes

Honey Garlic Dressing:

1	head garlic
1 tbsp	white wine vinegar
1½ tsp	liquid honey
1 tsp	Dijon mustard
¼ tsp	salt
Pinch	pepper
2 tbsp	extra-virgin olive oil
2 tbsp	vegetable oil

Makes 8 servings.
PER SERVING: about 52 cal, I g pro, 4 g total fat (I g sat. fat), 5 g carb, I g fibre, 0 mg chol, 89 mg sodium. % RDI: 3% calcium, 5% iron, II% vit A, 20% vit C, 9% folate.

ROMAINE SALAD
with lemon caper dressing

THIS SIMPLE SALAD IS GREAT FOR TAKING TO POTLUCKS, BECAUSE IT'S MADE WITH STURDY LETTUCES THAT DON'T WILT QUICKLY. THE KEY IS TO DRESS IT RIGHT BEFORE YOU BRING IT TO THE TABLE.

50

INGREDIENTS

6 cups	chopped romaine lettuce
2 cups	torn radicchio
1	small sweet onion, thinly sliced
½ cup	crumbled feta cheese

Lemon Caper Dressing:

2 tbsp	minced fresh parsley
2 tbsp	minced sweet onion
2 tbsp	extra-virgin olive oil
2 tbsp	vegetable oil
2 tbsp	lemon juice
1 tsp	drained rinsed capers
¼ tsp	each salt and pepper
¼ tsp	granulated sugar

METHOD

Lemon Caper Dressing: In small food processor or blender, purée together parsley, onion, olive oil, vegetable oil, lemon juice, capers, salt, pepper and sugar until fairly smooth.

In large bowl, combine romaine lettuce, radicchio and onion; sprinkle with feta cheese. Toss with dressing just before serving.

If you are taking this salad to a party, make the dressing and refrigerate it in an airtight jar. Give it a good shake or whisk to re-emulsify it before adding it to the greens.

Makes 8 servings.
PER SERVING: about 106 cal, 2 g pro, 9 g total fat (2 g sat. fat), 5 g carb, 1 g fibre, 9 mg chol, 196 mg sodium, 173 mg potassium. % RDI: 6% calcium, 5% iron, 23% vit A, 22% vit C, 30% folate.

MIXED GREENS
with pomegranate vinaigrette

INSTEAD OF PREMIXED GREENS, LOOK FOR A VARIETY, SUCH AS FRISÉE, RADICCHIO AND BABY SPINACH OR ROMAINE LEAVES, TO CREATE YOUR OWN SIGNATURE MIXTURE. FOR A GUIDE TO WASHING AND STORING GREENS, SEE PAGE 24.

INGREDIENTS

6 cups	lightly packed mixed greens
4 cups	lightly packed trimmed arugula
1	head Belgian endive, separated in leaves
1 cup	thinly sliced celery
⅓ cup	dried cranberries
⅓ cup	pomegranate seeds (see how-to, page 39)

Spicy Candied Pecans:

2 tbsp	granulated sugar
2 tbsp	corn syrup
Pinch	each salt, cinnamon, ground ginger and cayenne pepper
½ cup	pecan halves

Pomegranate Vinaigrette:

3 tbsp	bottled pomegranate juice
2 tbsp	red wine vinegar
1	shallot, finely chopped
1 tsp	liquid honey
¼ tsp	salt
¼ tsp	Dijon mustard
2 tbsp	olive oil

METHOD

Spicy Candied Pecans: In small saucepan, bring 2 tbsp water, sugar, corn syrup, salt, cinnamon, ginger and cayenne pepper to boil over medium heat. Boil until syrupy and reduced by half, 2 to 4 minutes. Stir in pecans to coat.

Transfer to parchment paper–lined baking sheet; using fork, separate into single layer. Bake in 325°F (160°C) oven until golden and fragrant, 7 to 9 minutes. Let cool. (*Make-ahead: Store in airtight container for up to 3 days.*)

Pomegranate Vinaigrette: In large bowl, whisk together pomegranate juice, vinegar, shallot, honey, salt and mustard; slowly whisk in oil until emulsified. (*Make-ahead: Refrigerate in airtight container for up to 2 days.*)

Add mixed greens, arugula, Belgian endive, celery, cranberries and pomegranate seeds to dressing; toss to coat. Sprinkle with candied pecans.

TEST KITCHEN TIP

The pecans that garnish this salad are so tasty that you might want to make extra to munch on as an appetizer. Or just make them on their own for an addictive treat anytime.

Makes 6 servings.

PER SERVING: about 187 cal, 2 g pro, 11 g total fat (1 g sat. fat), 23 g carb, 3 g fibre, 0 mg chol, 142 mg sodium, 368 mg potassium. % RDI: 7% calcium, 7% iron, 16% vit A, 18% vit C, 34% folate.

BACON, ROQUEFORT AND ROMAINE SALAD

HOMEMADE GARLIC CROUTONS, JUICY TOMATOES AND CHUNKS OF FLAVOURFUL BLUE CHEESE
GIVE CRISP ROMAINE LETTUCE TRUE STEAKHOUSE ALLURE. YOU MAY NOT NORMALLY BE A FAN OF ANCHOVIES,
BUT THEY'RE ONE OF THE KEYS TO THE DRESSING'S SALTY (BUT NOT FISHY) APPEAL.

53

METHOD

Anchovy Dressing: Whisk together oil, vinegar, anchovy paste, garlic, pepper, Worcestershire sauce and salt. *(Make-ahead: Cover and refrigerate for up to 24 hours.)*

Garlic Croutons: Toss together bread cubes, oil, garlic, salt and pepper. Bake on rimmed baking sheet in 400°F (200°C) oven until golden, about 12 minutes. Let cool. *(Make-ahead: Store in airtight container for up to 24 hours.)*

In large bowl, toss lettuce with dressing to coat. Add croutons, bacon, tomatoes and Roquefort cheese; gently toss to combine.

INGREDIENTS

12 cups	torn romaine lettuce
4	slices bacon, cooked and chopped
1 cup	halved cherry or grape tomatoes
½ cup	crumbled Roquefort cheese or other blue cheese

Anchovy Dressing:

3 tbsp	extra-virgin olive oil
1 tbsp	white wine vinegar
1½ tsp	anchovy paste (see tip, page 37)
1	clove garlic, minced
¼ tsp	pepper
¼ tsp	Worcestershire sauce
Pinch	salt

Garlic Croutons:

3 cups	cubed (¾ inch/2 cm) French or Italian bread
2 tbsp	extra-virgin olive oil
1	clove garlic, minced
Pinch	each salt and pepper

Local blue cheeses are a tasty alternative to French Roquefort; for a Canadian twist, try Bleu Bénédictin or L'Ermite from Quebec. Both are creamy and have a strong blue flavour that matches well with the smoky bacon and slightly salty anchovy dressing.

Makes 8 servings.
PER SERVING: about 172 cal, 5 g pro, 13 g total fat (3 g sat. fat), 9 g carb, 2 g fibre, 12 mg chol, 331 mg sodium. % RDI: 8% calcium, 9% iron, 45% vit A, 33% vit C, 50% folate.

RADICCHIO AND ARUGULA SALAD
with goat cheese and pears

WITH THEIR SWEETNESS AND CHEWY TEXTURE, PRUNES MAKE A SURPRISINGLY TOOTHSOME ADDITION TO THIS AUTUMN SALAD. THE COMBINATION OF EARTHY, SWEET, NUTTY AND TANGY ELEMENTS IS IN PERFECT HARMONY.

METHOD

In large bowl, toss together radicchio, arugula, red onion, pear, prunes, pecans and chives.

Grainy Mustard Dressing: Whisk together vinegar, oil, mustard, salt, pepper and sugar. Pour over salad; toss to coat. Sprinkle with goat cheese.

INGREDIENTS

2	heads radicchio, torn
4 cups	lightly packed baby arugula
Half	red onion, thinly sliced
1	pear, cored and cut in thin wedges
15	pitted prunes, halved
¾ cup	toasted pecan pieces (see how-to, below)
3 tbsp	finely chopped fresh chives
115 g	soft goat cheese, crumbled (about 1 cup)

Grainy Mustard Dressing:

2 tbsp	red wine vinegar
2 tbsp	extra-virgin olive oil
4 tsp	grainy mustard
¼ tsp	each salt and pepper
Pinch	granulated sugar

HOW TO

TOAST PECANS

Spread pecans in single layer on rimmed baking sheet; toast in 325°F (160°C) oven until fragrant, 4 to 6 minutes. Or, for small amounts, toast in dry skillet over medium heat, shaking often, for 3 to 5 minutes.

Makes 8 servings.

PER SERVING: about 212 cal, 5 g pro, 14 g total fat (3 g sat. fat), 19 g carb, 4 g fibre, 7 mg chol, 170 mg sodium, 391 mg potassium. % RDI: 6% calcium, 11% iron, 10% vit A, 12% vit C, 21% folate.

MEDITERRANEAN KALE SALAD

MARINATING KALE HELPS SOFTEN THE HEARTY CRUCIFEROUS GREENS
WHILE ADDING FLAVOUR. USE A SHARP VEGETABLE PEELER
TO SHAVE THE CHEESE INTO THE COLOURFUL SALAD.

INGREDIENTS

3 tbsp	extra-virgin olive oil
2 tbsp	balsamic vinegar
1 tsp	liquid honey
2	cloves garlic, minced
½ tsp	pepper
Pinch	salt
10 cups	stemmed kale (see how-to, page 46), thinly sliced
2 cups	cherry tomatoes, halved
1	can (398 mL) water-packed artichoke hearts, drained, rinsed and thinly sliced
1 cup	shaved Pecorino-Romano or Parmesan cheese (about 80 g)

METHOD

In large bowl, whisk together oil, vinegar, honey, garlic, pepper and salt.

Add kale, cherry tomatoes and artichoke hearts; toss to coat. Cover and refrigerate, tossing occasionally, until kale begins to soften slightly, about 2 hours. *(Make-ahead: Refrigerate for up to 24 hours.)*

Toss kale mixture; sprinkle with Pecorino-Romano cheese.

Makes 8 to 10 servings.

PER EACH OF 10 SERVINGS: about 125 cal, 6 g pro, 7 g total fat (2 g sat. fat), 12 g carb, 3 g fibre, 8 mg chol, 213 mg sodium, 476 mg potassium. % RDI: 18% calcium, 12% iron, 64% vit A, 145% vit C, 17% folate.

In-Season Vegetables

Veggies are best enjoyed at their peak ripeness. This list will help you make the most of them when they're available in farmer's markets or grocery stores. For In-Season Fruits, turn to page 255.

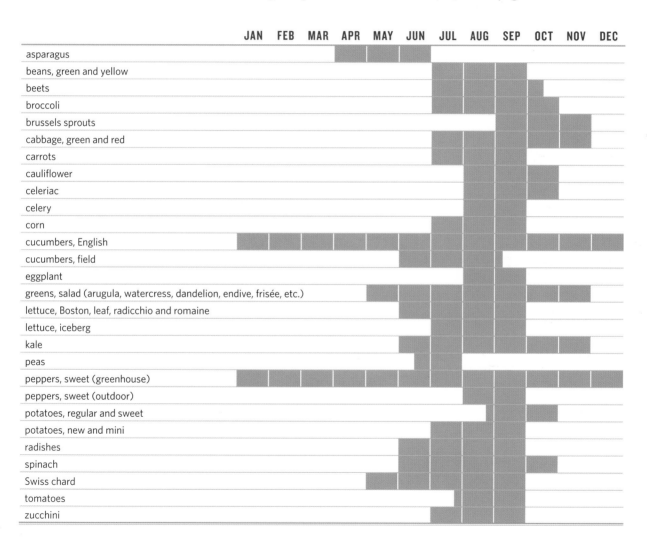

ROASTED BEET AND FETA SALAD

BRINY FETA CHEESE IS STRONG ENOUGH TO TAKE ON THE SWEET,
EARTHY FLAVOUR OF ROASTED BEETS IN THIS HARVESTTIME SIDE DISH. BABY BEETS ARE
ESPECIALLY TENDER, SO THEY'RE A TERRIFIC CHOICE FOR SALADS.

METHOD

Wrap beets in double-thickness square of foil; roast on baking sheet in 425°F (220°C) oven until tender, about 45 minutes. Let cool enough to handle. Remove skins; cut beets into wedges. Set aside.

In large bowl, whisk together oil, vinegar, mustard, salt and pepper. Add greens, red onion, parsley, dill, chives and beets; toss to coat. Sprinkle with feta cheese.

INGREDIENTS

6	baby beets, trimmed
3 tbsp	extra-virgin olive oil
2 tbsp	red wine vinegar
½ tsp	Dijon mustard
Pinch	each salt and pepper
6 cups	loosely packed baby greens
¼ cup	thinly sliced red onion
2 tbsp	chopped fresh parsley
2 tbsp	chopped fresh dill
2 tbsp	chopped fresh chives
½ cup	crumbled feta cheese

Makes 4 servings.

PER SERVING: about 184 cal, 5 g pro, 15 g total fat (4 g sat. fat), 10 g carb, 3 g fibre, 17 mg chol, 287 mg sodium, 466 mg potassium. % RDI: 15% calcium, 11% iron, 23% vit A, 30% vit C, 59% folate.

60

HEARTY DINNER

RECIPES

UPDATED CHICKEN CAESAR

NOT YOUR TRADITIONAL CAESAR, THIS SALAD IS MODERNIZED WITH A LITTLE TWIST:
IT'S COMPOSED RATHER THAN TOSSED, MEANING IT IS ARRANGED DECORATIVELY ON THE PLATE.
THIS IS A HEARTY MEAL THAT'S BEAUTIFUL FOR CASUAL ENTERTAINING.

INGREDIENTS

4	boneless skinless chicken breasts (450 g)
4 tsp	extra-virgin olive oil
2 tsp	Montreal Steak Spice
2	romaine lettuce hearts
⅓ cup	shaved Parmesan cheese

Caesar Vinaigrette:

1½ tsp	grated lemon zest
¼ cup	lemon juice
¼ cup	extra-virgin olive oil
3 tbsp	red wine vinegar
4	anchovy fillets, minced
1	clove garlic, minced
Pinch	each salt and pepper

METHOD

Toss chicken with half of the oil and the steak spice; let stand for 10 minutes.

In large skillet, heat remaining oil over medium-high heat; cook chicken, turning once, until golden and no longer pink inside, 8 to 10 minutes. Let stand for 5 minutes; thinly slice crosswise.

Meanwhile, trim root end of each romaine heart, leaving core intact. Quarter each heart lengthwise through core.

Caesar Vinaigrette: Whisk together lemon zest, lemon juice, oil, vinegar, anchovies, garlic, salt and pepper. Arrange two romaine quarters on each of four plates; top with chicken. Drizzle with vinaigrette; sprinkle with Parmesan cheese.

Montreal Steak Spice is a blend of herbs and spices typically used to season steak and other meats. The story is that it originated as a variation on the dry rub used to make Montreal-style smoked meat. The blend can vary slightly depending on the maker, but it generally contains black and red pepper, salt, garlic, onion, dill, mustard and a variety of herbs. You can find ready-made bottles of it in the seasonings section of the supermarket and in bulk stores.

Makes 4 servings.

PER SERVING: about 406 cal, 38 g pro, 23 g total fat (4 g sat. fat), 13 g carb, 7 g fibre, 87 mg chol, 479 mg sodium, 1,200 mg potassium. % RDI: 18% calcium, 29% iron, 274% vit A, 138% vit C, 196% folate.

GRILLED BUFFALO CHICKEN SALAD
with blue cheese dressing

DO YOU WANT WINGS OR SALAD? TONIGHT, YOU CAN HAVE BOTH AT THE SAME TIME! HOT WINGS WITH BLUE CHEESE DIP—A PUB FAVOURITE—TAKE ON A NEW PERSONA IN THIS LIGHTENED-UP GRILLED CHICKEN SALAD. YOU CAN EVEN FOLD THE SALAD UP IN A TORTILLA FOR A PORTABLE DINNER ON A BUSY NIGHT.

METHOD

Grilled Buffalo Chicken: Stir hot sauce with butter; remove 2 tbsp and set aside. Place chicken on greased grill over medium-high heat; close lid and grill, brushing with remaining sauce and turning once, until chicken is no longer pink inside, about 8 minutes. Let stand for 5 minutes; slice and toss with reserved sauce.

Blue Cheese Dressing: Meanwhile, whisk together buttermilk, blue cheese, yogurt, vinegar, sugar and pepper.

Divide lettuce, cucumber and carrot among four plates. Top with chicken; drizzle with dressing.

INGREDIENTS

8 cups	torn leaf lettuce
1 cup	sliced English cucumber
1	small carrot, shredded

Grilled Buffalo Chicken:

¼ cup	cayenne pepper–based hot sauce (such as Frank's RedHot)
2 tbsp	butter, melted
450 g	boneless skinless chicken cutlets

Blue Cheese Dressing:

⅓ cup	buttermilk
¼ cup	crumbled blue cheese
3 tbsp	2% plain yogurt
1 tbsp	cider vinegar
¼ tsp	granulated sugar
Pinch	pepper

Makes 4 servings.

PER SERVING: about 219 cal, 30 g pro, 7 g total fat (4 g sat. fat), 7 g carb, 2 g fibre, 83 mg chol, 486 mg sodium, 629 mg potassium. % RDI: 12% calcium, 9% iron, 78% vit A, 25% vit C, 18% folate.

GRILLED CHICKEN CLUB SALAD

WITH ALL THE FLAVOURS OF A CLUB SANDWICH, THIS SALAD MAKES A HEARTY SUPPER. IT'S ALSO EXCELLENT TO BRING TO A BARBECUE WITH FRIENDS; TRANSPORT THE MARINATED CHICKEN AND OTHER INGREDIENTS IN SEPARATE CONTAINERS, THEN SKEWER, GRILL AND ASSEMBLE THE SALAD FRESH AT THE PARTY.

INGREDIENTS

750 g	boneless skinless chicken breasts
Half	red onion
12	slices bacon
24	cherry tomatoes
Pinch	each salt and pepper
6 cups	torn romaine lettuce
1½ cups	croutons (such as Parmesan Croutons, page 66)

Creamy Herbed Dressing:

2 tbsp	minced fresh parsley
2 tbsp	light mayonnaise
2 tbsp	white wine vinegar
4 tsp	grainy or Dijon mustard
½ tsp	dried basil
¼ tsp	each salt and pepper
⅔ cup	vegetable oil

METHOD

Creamy Herbed Dressing: In small bowl, whisk together parsley, mayonnaise, vinegar, mustard, basil, salt and pepper; slowly whisk in oil until emulsified. *(Make-ahead: Cover and refrigerate for up to 4 days.)*

Cut chicken into thirty-six 1-inch (2.5 cm) cubes; place in bowl. Add half of the dressing; toss to coat. Cover and refrigerate for 30 minutes.

Cut red onion into twenty-four 1½-inch (4 cm) pieces. Cut each bacon slice crosswise into thirds. Wrap one bacon piece around each chicken cube. Onto each of 12 metal or soaked 10-inch (25 cm) wooden skewers, thread one chicken cube, one piece red onion and one tomato. Repeat once. Finish with third chicken cube. Sprinkle with salt and pepper.

Place skewers on greased grill over medium heat; close lid and grill, turning three times, until bacon is crisp and chicken is no longer pink inside, about 12 minutes.

Mound lettuce and croutons on six plates; top each with two skewers. Drizzle with remaining dressing.

Makes 6 servings.
PER SERVING: about 435 cal, 32 g pro, 28 g total fat (4 g sat. fat), 13 g carb, 2 g fibre, 78 mg chol, 462 mg sodium. % RDI: 4% calcium, 15% iron, 19% vit A, 47% vit C, 45% folate.

Croûtes, Crostini and Croutons

Salads are always more enticing with an interesting garnish on top.
These three additions give you flavour, crunch and visual appeal.

SALT AND PEPPER CROÛTES

A ficelle is shorter and narrower than a regular baguette, making it the perfect bread for one-bite croûtes. If you can't find a ficelle, use half a regular baguette and cut it in half lengthwise before slicing.

1	ficelle
¼ cup	extra-virgin olive oil
1½ tsp	coarse sea salt
½ tsp	coarsely ground pepper

Cut ficelle into ¼-inch (5 mm) thick slices; arrange on rimmed baking sheet. Brush with half of the oil; sprinkle with half each of the salt and pepper.

Bake in 350°F (180°C) oven for 15 minutes. Turn and brush with remaining oil; sprinkle with remaining salt and pepper. Bake until golden and crisp, about 10 minutes. Let cool. (*Make-ahead: Store in airtight container for up to 2 weeks.*)

Makes about 60 pieces.
PER PIECE: about 13 cal, trace pro, 1 g total fat (trace sat. fat), 1 g carb, 0 g fibre, 0 mg chol, 50 mg sodium. % RDI: 1% iron.

EASY CROSTINI

These simple toasted baguette slices are ultracrunchy and slightly garlicky—perfect atop a simple Caesar or green salad.

1	baguette
2 tbsp	extra-virgin olive oil
1	clove garlic, halved

Cut baguette into 24 slices; brush with oil. Broil on rimmed baking sheet until golden, about 4 minutes. Rub with cut sides of garlic. (*Make-ahead: Store in airtight container for up to 2 days.*)

Makes 24 pieces.
PER PIECE: about 44 cal, 1 g pro, 1 g total fat (trace sat. fat), 7 g carb, trace fibre, 0 mg chol, 77 mg sodium, 15 mg potassium. % RDI: 3% iron, 7% folate.

PARMESAN CROUTONS

It may seem crazy to spring for real Parmigiano-Reggiano for these salad toppers, but the flavour is unbelievable. Of course, less-pricey Parmesan or grana Padano cheese makes a great substitute.

2 cups	cubed (¼ inch/5 mm) day-old bread
⅓ cup	grated Parmigiano-Reggiano cheese
2 tbsp	extra-virgin olive oil
¼ tsp	crumbled dried thyme
Pinch	salt
Pinch	cayenne pepper

Toss together bread cubes, Parmigiano-Reggiano cheese, oil, thyme, salt and cayenne pepper; spread on rimmed baking sheet. Bake in 350°F (180°C) oven until golden and crisp, 10 minutes. Let cool. (*Make-ahead: Store in airtight container for up to 5 days.*)

Makes about 2 cups.
PER 2 TBSP: about 35 cal, 1 g pro, 2 g total fat (1 g sat. fat), 2 g carb, trace fibre, 2 mg chol, 54 mg sodium, 8 mg potassium. % RDI: 3% calcium, 1% iron, 2% folate.

CHICKEN, PEACH AND SPINACH SALAD

WHEN PEACHES ARE IN SEASON AT THE END OF SUMMER, THIS DINNER SALAD IS ANOTHER TASTY WAY TO USE THEM UP AS THEY HIT THE PERFECT RIPENESS. THEIR SWEETNESS BLENDS SO NICELY WITH THE LICORICE-FLAVOURED FENNEL AND TENDER SPINACH.

METHOD

In small bowl, stir together garlic, lemon zest, thyme, salt and pepper; stir in oil until blended. Brush all over chicken; let stand for 15 minutes.

Place chicken on greased grill over medium-high heat; close lid and grill, turning once, until no longer pink inside, about 15 minutes. Thinly slice.

Champagne Vinaigrette: In large bowl, whisk together oil, vinegar, sugar, salt and pepper.

Add spinach, fennel, onion, peaches and chicken to vinaigrette; toss to coat.

INGREDIENTS

2	cloves garlic, minced
2 tsp	finely grated lemon zest
1 tsp	chopped fresh thyme (or ¼ tsp dried)
½ tsp	each salt and pepper
2 tbsp	extra-virgin olive oil
2	boneless skinless chicken breasts
1	pkg (170 g) baby spinach
1 cup	thinly sliced cored fennel bulb
⅓ cup	thinly sliced red onion
3	peaches, peeled, pitted and sliced

Champagne Vinaigrette:

3 tbsp	extra-virgin olive oil
2 tbsp	champagne vinegar or white wine vinegar
½ tsp	granulated sugar
¼ tsp	each salt and pepper

Makes 4 servings.

PER SERVING: about 279 cal, 18 g pro, 18 g total fat (3 g sat. fat), 12 g carb, 3 g fibre, 39 mg chol, 512 mg sodium. % RDI: 6% calcium, 15% iron, 43% vit A, 35% vit C, 43% folate.

CRISPY TORTILLA ANCHO CHICKEN SALAD

ANCHO CHILI POWDER HAS A KICK. FOR SENSITIVE PALATES,
SUBSTITUTE CHILI POWDER, WHICH IS MUCH MILDER. SERVE THIS HEARTY SOUTHWESTERN-STYLE
SALAD WITH A DOLLOP OF SOUR CREAM TO COOL THINGS OFF.

INGREDIENTS

3	small flour tortillas, halved and cut crosswise in ½-inch (1 cm) wide strips
1 tbsp	vegetable oil
450 g	boneless skinless chicken breasts, cut in ¾-inch (2 cm) cubes
1	sweet pepper, chopped
2	cloves garlic, minced
1¼ tsp	ancho chili powder
¼ tsp	pepper
Pinch	salt
1 cup	rinsed drained canned black beans
½ cup	frozen corn kernels
2	green onions, chopped
1 tbsp	lime juice
4 cups	torn leaf lettuce
½ cup	shredded old Cheddar cheese
1	avocado, pitted, peeled and chopped

Honey Lime Dressing:

3 tbsp	olive oil
2 tbsp	lime juice
2 tsp	liquid honey
Pinch	salt

METHOD

Toss tortilla strips with 1 tsp of the oil. In large nonstick skillet, cook strips over medium-high heat, tossing often, until golden, about 2 minutes. Transfer to bowl.

Add remaining oil to skillet; cook chicken, sweet pepper, garlic, chili powder, pepper and salt, stirring often, until chicken is no longer pink inside, about 4 minutes.

Stir in beans, corn, green onions and lime juice; cook until warmed through, about 3 minutes.

Honey Lime Dressing: In large bowl, whisk together oil, lime juice, honey and salt.

Add lettuce to dressing; toss to coat. Spoon chicken mixture over lettuce mixture; sprinkle with cheese and avocado. Garnish with tortilla strips.

Makes 4 servings.

PER SERVING: about 539 cal, 36 g pro, 29 g total fat (6 g sat. fat), 35 g carb, 9 g fibre, 81 mg chol, 496 mg sodium, 958 mg potassium. % RDI: 14% calcium, 22% iron, 36% vit A, 63% vit C, 56% folate.

MANGO CHICKEN SALAD
with thai-style vinaigrette

THAI MANGO SALAD IS USUALLY SERVED AS A SIDE DISH, BUT WITH THE ADDITION OF COOKED CHICKEN, IT BECOMES THE MAIN EVENT. THIS IS A GREAT RECIPE TO TRY WHEN YOU HAVE READY-MADE ROTISSERIE CHICKEN IN THE FRIDGE.

70

INGREDIENTS

6 cups	loosely packed mixed greens
3 cups	shredded cooked chicken
1	firm ripe mango, peeled, pitted and sliced (see how-to, page 257)
1 cup	cherry or grape tomatoes, quartered
¼ cup	chopped fresh cilantro
⅓ cup	unsalted dry-roasted peanuts, coarsely chopped

Thai-Style Vinaigrette:

3 tbsp	vegetable oil
2 tbsp	lime juice
2 tsp	packed brown sugar
2 tsp	fish sauce
½ tsp	Asian chili sauce (such as sriracha)

METHOD

Thai-Style Vinaigrette: Whisk together oil, lime juice, brown sugar, fish sauce and Asian chili sauce.

In large bowl, toss together mixed greens, chicken, mango, cherry tomatoes and cilantro. Add vinaigrette; gently toss to coat. Sprinkle with peanuts.

TEST KITCHEN TIP

Thai mango salads are usually made with slightly underripe, green mangoes, which are a bit on the tart side. For this salad, riper fruit is in order. Look for mangoes that just yield to the pressure of fingers, which means they are sweet but not overripe.

Makes 4 servings.
PER SERVING: about 431 cal, 36 g pro, 25 g total fat (4 g sat. fat), 18 g carb, 4 g fibre, 95 mg chol, 355 mg sodium, 777 mg potassium. % RDI: 8% calcium, 17% iron, 27% vit A, 52% vit C, 50% folate.

GRILLED VEGETABLE AND CHICKEN SALAD

WE'VE USED HEARTY GREEN LEAF LETTUCE IN THIS DINNER SALAD FOR TWO BECAUSE IT
WON'T WILT AS QUICKLY AS MIXED BABY GREENS OR BOSTON LETTUCE. GRILLED
EGGPLANT IS ANOTHER APPETIZING VEGETABLE YOU CAN ADD IF YOU LIKE.

METHOD

Stir together vinegar, oil, garlic and half each of the salt and pepper. Remove 2 tbsp and set aside for basting vegetables.

Sprinkle chicken with remaining salt and pepper. Place on greased grill over medium-high heat; close lid and grill, turning once, until chicken is no longer pink inside, about 12 minutes. Let stand for 5 minutes before slicing.

Meanwhile, add red pepper, mushroom and zucchini to grill; grill, covered, turning and basting with reserved dressing, until tender, about 6 minutes. Transfer to cutting board; slice. Let cool, about 10 minutes.

Divide lettuce, grilled vegetables and chicken between two bowls. Drizzle with remaining dressing; toss to combine.

INGREDIENTS

¼ cup	balsamic vinegar
¼ cup	extra-virgin olive oil
1	clove garlic, minced
¼ tsp	each salt and pepper
1	boneless skinless chicken breast (about 225 g)
1	sweet red pepper, quartered
1	large portobello mushroom, halved
1	large zucchini, sliced lengthwise
4 cups	chopped leaf lettuce

HOW TO

TAKE THIS SALAD ON THE RUN

This salad makes a great dinner to take with you on busy nights. (It's so much better than the food you can get around a baseball diamond.) In two 3-cup airtight containers, arrange lettuce, grilled vegetables and grilled chicken. Pour remaining dressing into small airtight container (you can refrigerate it for up to 24 hours). To serve, drizzle dressing over salad; shake or toss to combine.

Makes 2 servings.

PER SERVING: about 455 cal, 30 g pro, 29 g total fat (4 g sat. fat), 19 g carb, 5 g fibre, 67 mg chol, 382 mg sodium, 1,115 mg potassium. % RDI: 6% calcium, 18% iron, 86% vit A, 197% vit C, 31% folate.

SPINACH SALAD
with chicken and fruit

PEPPERY WATERCRESS AND PIQUANT ONION HARMONIZE WITH SWEET FRUIT IN THIS WELL-BALANCED MEAL.
ALMONDS ARE A TASTY, CRUNCHY TOPPING, BUT ANY NUTS WILL WORK EQUALLY WELL AS A GARNISH.

METHOD

Mint Poppy Seed Dressing: Whisk together mint, olive oil, canola oil, vinegar, shallot, garlic, poppy seeds, salt and pepper.

In large bowl, toss together spinach, watercress, chicken, raspberries, blackberries, red onion, almonds and mango. Add dressing; toss to coat.

TEST KITCHEN TIP

Fresh raspberries and blackberries are delicate and require a little TLC to keep them at their best. Store unwashed berries in the fridge in their original packaging until you're ready to use them—usually no longer than a few days, since they spoil quickly. Running water can bruise the delicate berries. When you're ready to wash them, place them in a sieve or colander and dunk them in a sink full of cold water. Gently stir them with your hands to remove any grit. Then lift the berries out of the water, and lay them on a towel to dry. Don't return washed berries to the fridge, because they will deteriorate more quickly.

INGREDIENTS

6 cups	baby spinach
2 cups	trimmed watercress
1	boneless skinless chicken breast, cooked and sliced
½ cup	each fresh raspberries and blackberries (see tip, below)
½ cup	thinly sliced red onion
⅓ cup	slivered almonds
Half	mango, peeled, pitted and chopped (see how-to, page 257)

Mint Poppy Seed Dressing:

2 tbsp	chopped fresh mint
2 tbsp	extra-virgin olive oil
2 tbsp	canola oil
2 tbsp	red wine vinegar
1 tbsp	minced shallot
1	small clove garlic, minced
1 tsp	poppy seeds
Pinch	each salt and pepper

Makes 4 servings.
PER SERVING: about 271 cal, 13 g pro, 19 g total fat (2 g sat. fat), 14 g carb, 5 g fibre, 21 mg chol, 65 mg sodium. % RDI: 11% calcium, 19% iron, 62% vit A, 62% vit C, 51% folate.

APRICOT, CHICKEN AND ALMOND SALAD

THE SWEET AND SAVOURY COMBINATION OF CHICKEN, DRIED FRUIT AND FETA CHEESE MAKES FOR A WONDERFUL LIGHT MEAL. VARY THE FRUIT AND THE CHEESE FOR TOTALLY DIFFERENT TAKES ON THIS CLASSIC DINNER SALAD.

INGREDIENTS

2 tbsp	olive oil (approx)
2	boneless skinless chicken breasts
2 tsp	balsamic vinegar
Pinch	each salt and pepper
2 cups	torn Boston lettuce
⅓ cup	cubed feta cheese
⅓ cup	chopped dried apricots
¼ cup	sliced almonds, toasted (see tip, page 44)

METHOD

Brush nonstick skillet lightly with olive oil; heat over medium-high heat. Cook chicken, turning once, until no longer pink inside, 10 to 12 minutes. Let cool; dice. Transfer to large bowl.

Whisk together remaining 2 tbsp olive oil, balsamic vinegar, salt and pepper until well combined.

Add lettuce, feta cheese, apricots and almonds to chicken. Drizzle dressing over top; toss to coat.

HOW TO

SELECT FETA CHEESE FOR A DISH

Feta cheese originally comes from Greece and has now achieved protected status in the European Union. Only feta made in Greece from a blend of sheep's and goat's milk can be labelled as such in Europe. And while other countries legally can't use the name, they still make crumbly, brined feta-style cheeses, some even with cow's milk (though EU laws firmly forbid it in the real thing). In Canada, the name is considered generic, so cheesemakers are still using it on packaging. Cow's milk feta is softer and creamier but a bit more sour than Greek or Bulgarian feta, both of which are predominantly made from sheep's milk. Try different types to find your favourite.

Makes 2 servings.

PER SERVING: about 453 cal, 37 g pro, 26 g total fat (6 g sat. fat), 19 g carb, 3 g fibre, 95 mg chol, 302 mg sodium, 865 mg potassium. % RDI: 15% calcium, 18% iron, 29% vit A, 7% vit C, 25% folate.

NAPA CABBAGE SLAW
with grilled chicken

LEFTOVERS OF THIS CRUNCHY SUMMER SALAD ARE EXCELLENT FOR LUNCH THE NEXT DAY.
TO SCOOP OUT THE CUCUMBER SEEDS, HALVE THE CUCUMBER, THEN RUN A SPOON DOWN THE CENTRE.

INGREDIENTS

2	boneless skinless chicken breasts (about 450 g total)
Pinch	each salt and pepper
4 cups	lightly packed shredded napa cabbage
1	carrot, grated or julienned (see how-to, page 36)
1	sweet red pepper, thinly sliced
1	rib celery, thinly sliced diagonally
Half	English cucumber, halved lengthwise, seeded and thinly sliced diagonally
2	green onions, thinly sliced
⅓ cup	sliced almonds, toasted (see tip, page 44)

Soy Vinaigrette:

2 tbsp	vegetable oil
4 tsp	unseasoned rice vinegar
1 tbsp	sodium-reduced soy sauce
2 tsp	sesame oil
Pinch	salt

METHOD

Sprinkle chicken with salt and pepper. Place on greased grill over medium-high heat; close lid and grill, turning once, until no longer pink inside, 12 to 15 minutes. Let stand for 5 minutes before slicing.

Soy Vinaigrette: Meanwhile, in large bowl, whisk together vegetable oil, vinegar, soy sauce, sesame oil and salt.

Add cabbage, carrot, red pepper, celery, cucumber and green onions to vinaigrette; toss to coat. Top with chicken; sprinkle with almonds.

CHANGE IT UP
CREAMY TAHINI SLAW WITH GRILLED CHICKEN

Replace soy vinaigrette with a mixture of 2 tbsp olive oil, 4 tsp lemon juice, 1 tbsp tahini, 1 tbsp Balkan-style plain yogurt and ¼ tsp each salt and pepper.

Makes 4 servings.
PER SERVING: about 293 cal, 30 g pro, 15 g total fat (2 g sat. fat), 11 g carb, 3 g fibre, 67 mg chol, 242 mg sodium, 786 mg potassium. % RDI: 10% calcium, 11% iron, 40% vit A, 123% vit C, 39% folate.

No-Fail Creamy Dressings

Bottled salad dressing is full of additives and never tastes as nice as homemade.
With these easy options, you'll never need to buy it again.

CREAMY FETA-YOGURT DRESSING

Inspired by a dressing made at Bullock's Bistro in Yellowknife's Old Town, this creamy creation is so good you'll crave it forever.

½ cup	crumbled feta cheese
1	small clove garlic, grated or pressed
¼ cup	2% plain Greek yogurt
1 tbsp	extra-virgin olive oil
1 tbsp	lemon juice
1 tsp	liquid honey
Pinch	pepper

In bowl and using fork, mash feta cheese with garlic until in coarse crumbs. Stir in yogurt, oil, lemon juice, honey and pepper.

Makes about ⅔ cup.
PER I TBSP: about 36 cal, 2 g pro, 3 g total fat (I g sat. fat), I g carb, 0 g fibre, 7 mg chol, 82 mg sodium, 14 mg potassium. % RDI: 4% calcium, I% iron, I% vit A, I% folate.

THOUSAND ISLAND DRESSING

This classic dressing suits any mix of salad greens but is also tasty on simple lettuce wedges.

1 cup	light mayonnaise
2 tbsp	finely chopped sweet pickles
2 tbsp	each finely chopped drained capers and green olives
2 tbsp	ketchup or tomato-based chili sauce
2 tbsp	water
1 tbsp	cider vinegar
Pinch	pepper

In small bowl, whisk together mayonnaise, pickles, capers, green olives, ketchup, water, vinegar and pepper. (Make-ahead: Refrigerate in airtight container for up to 1 week.)

Makes about 1½ cups.
PER I TBSP: about 36 cal, trace pro, 3 g total fat (I g sat. fat), 2 g carb, 0 g fibre, 3 mg chol, 121 mg sodium. % RDI: 1% iron, 1% vit A.

CREAMY DILL RANCH DRESSING

Fresh dill gives this family-friendly dressing great flavour. You can use 1 tsp dried dillweed in a pinch.

⅔ cup	buttermilk
⅓ cup	light mayonnaise
2 tsp	cider vinegar
½ tsp	Dijon mustard
¼ tsp	pepper
Pinch	salt
Dash	hot pepper sauce
1 tbsp	each chopped fresh dill and parsley

In liquid measure or small bowl, whisk together buttermilk, mayonnaise, vinegar, mustard, pepper, salt and hot pepper sauce. Stir in dill and parsley. (Make-ahead: Refrigerate in airtight container for up to 3 days.)

Makes 1⅓ cups.
PER I TBSP: about 17 cal, trace pro, I g total fat (trace sat. fat), I g carb, 0 g fibre, 2 mg chol, 33 mg sodium. % RDI: 1% calcium.

COBB-STYLE SALAD

THIS TAKE ON CHEF'S SALAD—KNOWN FOR ITS COMBO OF BLUE CHEESE, HARD-COOKED EGG, CHICKEN, BACON, AVOCADO AND LETTUCE—IS BEAUTIFUL AS WELL AS HEARTY. USE WHATEVER TYPE OF BLUE CHEESE YOU PREFER, AND CHANGE IT UP WITH DIFFERENT LOCAL VARIETIES WHEN YOU CAN.

METHOD

Red Wine Vinaigrette: In bowl, whisk together oil, vinegar, lemon juice, Worcestershire sauce, salt, mustard, sugar, pepper and garlic. Pour into pitcher or jar; set aside.

Cover platter or large salad bowl with lettuce; top with watercress (if using). In rows on top of greens, arrange bacon, eggs, tomatoes, avocado and blue cheese. Scatter chives over top. Serve with dressing.

HOW TO

PERFECTLY HARD-COOK EGGS

Arrange eggs in single layer in saucepan; pour in enough cold water to come at least 1 inch (2.5 cm) above eggs. Cover and bring to boil over high heat. Immediately remove from heat; let stand for 12 minutes. Drain and chill eggs in cold water. Drain and peel off shells.

INGREDIENTS

4 cups	chopped iceberg and/or romaine lettuce
1 cup	chopped trimmed watercress (optional)
4	slices bacon, cooked and crumbled
4	hard-cooked eggs (see how-to, below), quartered
2	tomatoes, coarsely chopped
1	avocado, pitted, peeled and cubed
⅓ cup	crumbled blue cheese
2 tbsp	minced fresh chives or green onions

Red Wine Vinaigrette:

¼ cup	vegetable oil
2 tbsp	red wine vinegar
1 tsp	each lemon juice and Worcestershire sauce
½ tsp	each salt and dry mustard
¼ tsp	each granulated sugar and pepper
1	clove garlic, minced

Makes 4 to 6 servings.

PER EACH OF 6 SERVINGS: about 248 cal, 9 g pro, 21 g total fat (4 g sat. fat), 6 g carb, 3 g fibre, 134 mg chol, 452 mg sodium, 420 mg potassium. % RDI: 7% calcium, 8% iron, 12% vit A, 18% vit C, 34% folate.

PANCETTA AND EGG
on hearty greens

VERSIONS OF THIS SATISFYING SUPPER ARE TYPICALLY FOUND IN SMALL BISTROS ALL OVER FRANCE. FRESHLY GROUND BLACK PEPPER IS A VERY NICE ACCENT WHEN SPRINKLED OVER TOP.

80

INGREDIENTS

1 tbsp	extra-virgin olive oil
8	thin slices pancetta
1	pkg (340 g) mixed mushrooms, sliced
Pinch	each salt and pepper
1	head frisée, torn
1	head radicchio, torn
4	eggs, poached (see how-to, below)

Shallot Caper Dressing:

⅓ cup	thinly sliced shallots
2 tbsp	white wine vinegar
1 tbsp	drained capers, finely chopped
2 tsp	Dijon mustard
Pinch	granulated sugar
Pinch	each salt and pepper
⅓ cup	extra-virgin olive oil

METHOD

Shallot Caper Dressing: In bowl, stir together shallots, vinegar, capers, mustard, sugar, salt and pepper; slowly whisk in oil until emulsified. Set aside.

In large skillet, heat oil over medium-high heat; cook pancetta until crisp, about 4 minutes. Drain on paper towel–lined plate.

Drain all but 2 tbsp fat from pan; cook mushrooms, salt and pepper over medium heat, stirring occasionally, until tender and golden, about 6 minutes.

In large bowl, toss together frisée, radicchio, mushroom mixture and dressing. Divide among four plates; top each with pancetta and egg.

HOW TO
PERFECTLY POACH EGGS

In large saucepan or deep skillet, heat 2 to 3 inches (5 to 8 cm) water over medium heat until simmering. Add 1 tbsp vinegar. One at a time, crack eggs into custard cup or small bowl; gently slide into simmering water. Reduce heat to low; cook until whites are set and yolks are still runny, about 3 minutes. Using slotted spoon, transfer eggs to paper towel–lined tray; blot dry. Keep warm.

Makes 4 servings.

PER SERVING: about 395 cal, 16 g pro, 33 g total fat (6 g sat. fat), 13 g carb, 4 g fibre, 206 mg chol, 498 mg sodium, 976 mg potassium. % RDI: 11% calcium, 22% iron, 35% vit A, 22% vit C, 113% folate.

TURKEY SAUSAGE AND APPLE SALAD

TURKEY SAUSAGES ARE A MILDER ALTERNATIVE TO PORK SAUSAGES AND CAN BE LEANER (THOUGH IT PAYS TO CHECK THE NUTRITION LABEL TO BE SURE). HERE, THEY PAIR BEAUTIFULLY WITH SWEET APPLE AND SLIGHTLY BITTER LETTUCES FOR A YUMMY ONE-DISH MEAL.

INGREDIENTS

450 g	mild Italian turkey sausages
¼ cup	extra-virgin olive oil
2 tbsp	cider vinegar
1 tsp	each Dijon mustard and liquid honey
¼ tsp	each salt and pepper
¼ tsp	dried thyme
6 cups	chopped loosely packed escarole
2 cups	chopped loosely packed frisée
1	carrot, grated
1	Gala apple, cored and thinly sliced
½ cup	sliced English cucumber
⅓ cup	walnuts, toasted (see how-to, page 209) and chopped
¼ cup	sliced red onion

METHOD

Broil or grill sausages over medium-high heat, turning occasionally, until browned and no longer pink in centre, 18 to 20 minutes. Slice thickly.

Meanwhile, in large bowl, whisk together oil, vinegar, mustard, honey, salt, pepper and thyme.

Add escarole, frisée, carrot, apple, cucumber, walnuts and red onion to dressing. Add sausage; toss to coat.

Makes 4 to 6 servings.

PER EACH OF 6 SERVINGS: about 278 cal, 16 g pro, 20 g total fat (3 g sat. fat), 10 g carb, 3 g fibre, 55 mg chol, 524 mg sodium, 521 mg potassium. % RDI: 6% calcium, 14% iron, 28% vit A, 12% vit C, 44% folate.

RICOTTA TARTLETS AND SALAD
with tarragon vinaigrette

SOUFFLE-LIKE TARTLETS ADD A LOVELY FRENCH ELEMENT TO THIS ELEGANT HERBED SALAD.
THEY ALSO MAKE SCRUMPTIOUS BASES FOR CANAPÉS AND ARE WONDERFUL FLOATED IN BOWLS OF CREAMY SOUP.

METHOD

Ricotta Tartlets: Grease 12 mini-muffin cups; sprinkle sides and bottoms with 2 tbsp of the Parmesan cheese to coat evenly. Set aside. In bowl, beat together ricotta cheese, egg white, remaining Parmesan cheese, thyme, flour, pepper, baking powder, and lavender (if using) until smooth. Spoon into prepared mini-muffin cups; smooth tops. Bake in 350°F (180°C) oven until puffed and cake tester inserted in centre of several comes out clean, about 20 minutes. Let cool in pan on rack for 5 minutes.

Tarragon Vinaigrette: In large bowl, whisk together tarragon vinegar, mustard, savory, salt and pepper; slowly whisk in oil until emulsified.

Add baby greens and chives to vinaigrette; toss to coat. Divide among six plates; top each with two tartlets.

INGREDIENTS

8 cups	mixed baby greens
¼ cup	finely chopped fresh chives or green onions

Ricotta Tartlets:

½ cup	grated Parmesan cheese
1 cup	ricotta cheese
1	egg white
1 tbsp	chopped fresh thyme
1 tbsp	all-purpose flour
¼ tsp	pepper
¼ tsp	baking powder
¼ tsp	crumbled dried lavender (optional)

Tarragon Vinaigrette:

1 tbsp	tarragon vinegar or white wine vinegar
1 tsp	Dijon mustard
¼ tsp	crumbled dried savory
Pinch	each salt and pepper
¼ cup	extra-virgin olive oil

Makes 6 servings.
PER SERVING: about 209 cal, 10 g pro, 17 g total fat (6 g sat. fat), 5 g carb, 1 g fibre, 28 mg chol, 212 mg sodium. % RDI: 22% calcium, 8% iron, 23% vit A, 20% vit C, 32% folate.

GRILLED HALLOUMI AND ASPARAGUS SALAD

THE STAR OF THIS SALAD IS HALLOUMI, A SALTY, TOOTHSOME CHEESE FROM CYPRUS THAT HOLDS ITS SHAPE PERFECTLY WHEN GRILLED OR PAN-FRIED. A LOAF OF CRUSTY BREAD IS ALL YOU NEED TO MAKE A COMPLETE MEAL.

INGREDIENTS

1	bunch (450 g) asparagus, trimmed (see how-to, page 175)
1	pkg (250 g) halloumi cheese, cut in ½-inch (1 cm) thick slices
1	head Boston lettuce, torn
4 cups	torn romaine lettuce
¾ cup	cherry tomatoes, halved
2 tbsp	olive oil
2 tsp	red wine vinegar
Pinch	each salt and pepper

METHOD

Place asparagus on greased grill over medium-high heat; close lid and grill, turning often, for 3 minutes.

Add halloumi cheese; grill, covered and turning once, until asparagus is tender and slightly grill-marked, and halloumi is grill-marked, about 4 minutes.

Meanwhile, on platter, combine Boston lettuce, romaine lettuce and cherry tomatoes. Whisk together oil, vinegar, salt and pepper; drizzle over salad. Toss to coat. Top with asparagus and halloumi cheese.

CHANGE IT UP

SKILLET HALLOUMI AND ASPARAGUS SALAD

In large nonstick skillet, heat 2 tsp vegetable oil over medium heat; cook asparagus until tender-crisp, about 10 minutes. Set aside. In same skillet over medium heat, cook halloumi, turning once, until golden, about 4 minutes. Continue with recipe.

Makes 4 servings.

PER SERVING: about 304 cal, 16 g pro, 24 g total fat (11 g sat. fat), 9 g carb, 3 g fibre, 63 mg chol, 769 mg sodium, 458 mg potassium. % RDI: 36% calcium, 13% iron, 86% vit A, 37% vit C, 98% folate.

CHEF'S DINNER SALAD
with french-style dressing

MIXED GREENS AND A FEW INGREDIENTS FROM THE DELI MAKE FAST WORK OF SUPPER. SUBSTITUTE WHATEVER DELI MEAT OR CHEESE YOU HAVE IN YOUR FRIDGE FOR THE TURKEY AND HAVARTI.

INGREDIENTS

1	pkg (140 g) mixed greens
2	ribs celery, thinly sliced
1	carrot, shredded
170 g	smoked turkey, cut in sticks or strips
1 cup	cubed garden vegetable or dill Havarti cheese
1 cup	halved grape tomatoes

French-Style Dressing:

2 tbsp	ketchup
2 tbsp	red wine vinegar
½ tsp	sweet paprika
¼ tsp	each dry mustard and pepper
Pinch	salt
¼ cup	olive oil

METHOD

French-Style Dressing: In small bowl, whisk together ketchup, vinegar, paprika, mustard, pepper and salt; slowly whisk in oil until emulsified.

In large bowl, toss together mixed greens, celery and carrot; drizzle with dressing. Toss to coat. Arrange turkey, Havarti cheese and tomatoes on top.

Serving this hearty dinner salad in one big bowl saves the work of making four individual chef's salads. It's a handy time-saver on busy weeknights when you don't have a minute to spare.

Makes 4 servings.

PER SERVING: about 339 cal, 14 g pro, 27 g total fat (10 g sat. fat), 10 g carb, 2 g fibre, 61 mg chol, 884 mg sodium, 490 mg potassium. % RDI: 24% calcium, 13% iron, 44% vit A, 28% vit C, 23% folate.

PANZANELLA SALAD
with poached eggs

DON'T THROW AWAY A STALE LOAF OF BREAD. DO AS THE TUSCANS DO, AND CELEBRATE IT WITH A BREAD SALAD. IT'S A CLASSIC AND TASTY WAY TO USE UP BREAD THAT'S TOO FIRM FOR MAKING SANDWICHES OR EATING OUT OF HAND.

METHOD

Spread bread cubes on rimmed baking sheet; drizzle with 2 tbsp of the oil. Bake in 350°F (180°C) oven, stirring once, until golden and crisp, about 15 minutes. Let cool.

In large bowl, whisk together remaining oil, vinegar, anchovies, shallots, garlic, capers, salt and pepper. Add tomatoes, cucumber, basil and croutons; toss to coat. Divide among four plates; serve topped with eggs.

INGREDIENTS

4 cups	cubed (1 inch/2.5 cm) crustless Italian or French loaf
⅓ cup	extra-virgin olive oil
3 tbsp	red wine vinegar
4	anchovy fillets, minced (see tip, page 37)
2	shallots, finely sliced
2	cloves garlic, minced
1 tbsp	capers, drained
Pinch	each salt and pepper
2 cups	halved cherry tomatoes
2 cups	cubed (1 inch/2.5 cm) seeded English cucumber
¼ cup	chopped fresh basil
4	eggs, poached (see how-to, page 80)

Makes 4 servings.

PER SERVING: about 353 cal, 11 g pro, 25 g total fat (4 g sat. fat), 22 g carb, 2 g fibre, 190 mg chol, 455 mg sodium, 418 mg potassium. % RDI: 8% calcium, 17% iron, 16% vit A, 22% vit C, 38% folate.

OVEN-POACHED SALMON SALAD
with mustard vinaigrette

THIS METHOD FOR POACHING SALMON FILLETS IS SUPEREASY AND CONSISTENTLY PRODUCES TENDER, MOIST RESULTS. BUYING SKINLESS FILLETS WILL SAVE YOU TIME AND EFFORT, BUT YOU CAN SKIN THEM YOURSELF IF YOU PREFER.

INGREDIENTS

4	skinless centre-cut salmon fillets (about 175 g each)
¼ tsp	each salt and pepper
1 tbsp	capers, drained and rinsed
1	lemon, thinly sliced
4	sprigs fresh thyme
450 g	new potatoes, scrubbed and halved
450 g	green beans
1 cup	grape tomatoes
6 cups	torn romaine lettuce
4	hard-cooked eggs (see how-to, page 79), quartered

Mustard Vinaigrette:

3 tbsp	extra-virgin olive oil
1 tbsp	white wine vinegar
2 tsp	lemon juice
2 tsp	Dijon mustard
1	shallot or green onion (white part only), minced
1 tsp	minced fresh thyme
¼ tsp	each salt and pepper
Pinch	granulated sugar

METHOD

Mustard Vinaigrette: In large bowl, whisk together oil, vinegar, lemon juice, mustard, shallot, thyme, salt, pepper and sugar; set aside.

Place fish in centre of large piece of parchment paper. Sprinkle with salt and pepper; top with capers, lemon and thyme. Fold paper over fish so edges match; double-fold and pinch all edges to seal packet. Roast on baking sheet in 450°F (230°C) oven until fish flakes easily when tested, 10 to 15 minutes.

Meanwhile, in saucepan of boiling salted water, cook potatoes until almost fork-tender, about 8 minutes.

Add beans; cook until tender, about 2 minutes. Drain and rinse under cold water; pat dry. Add to vinaigrette along with tomatoes; toss to coat.

Arrange lettuce on plates. Top with potato mixture, eggs and salmon; drizzle with any remaining vinaigrette.

Makes 4 servings.
PER SERVING: about 575 cal, 41 g pro, 32 g total fat (6 g sat. fat), 32 g carb, 7 g fibre, 270 mg chol, 978 mg sodium, 1,344 mg potassium. % RDI: 12% calcium, 25% iron, 59% vit A, 88% vit C, 96% folate.

How to Set Up a Salad Bar

A salad bar is an interesting option for a party. Your guests will enjoy choosing their favourites from a variety of ingredients, and the do-it-yourself aspect is fun for both adults and children.

Set out a stack of bowls or plates at the start, then the salad makings, with dressings and garnishes at the end. Make sure each ingredient has its own dedicated serving utensil, and try not to swap them between dishes—especially when they've been used on highly perishable items, such as creamy dressings, meats and cheeses.

Keep serving bowls cold by setting them in larger bowls filled with ice. It's always better to put out small bowls and replenish them as needed than to let larger bowls sit out for longer.

TO FEED EIGHT TO 10 PEOPLE, SET OUT THE FOLLOWING:

- 12 to 16 cups mixed greens, torn romaine lettuce or baby spinach (or a combination)
- 8 cups finely shredded red cabbage (about half a head)
- 1 each sweet red, yellow and orange pepper, diced
- 2 cups shredded carrot
- 2 cups sliced English cucumber
- 2 cups rinsed drained canned chickpeas
- 2 cups cubed feta, cubed Gouda or bocconcini cheese
- 2 cups grape or cherry tomatoes
- 1 cup thinly sliced green or red onions
- 1 cup thinly sliced radishes
- 1 cup drained oil-brined black olives
- ½ cup seeds or nuts (such as sunflower seeds, pepitas, pecans or walnuts)
- 1 cup each of two salad dressings: one creamy option, such as Creamy Dill Ranch Dressing (page 78), and one vinaigrette, such as Oregano Red Wine Vinaigrette (page 48) or Basic Berry Vinaigrette (page 148)

If this mix of flavours and textures isn't exactly what you want, let your imagination run wild. Use the proportions as a guideline, and add other favourite ingredients. (We recommend some chopped smoky bacon or croutons.) The only limitation is your creativity!

VEGETARIAN CHEF'S SALAD

CHEF'S SALADS ARE FILLING AND MAKE A TERRIFIC MEAL, BUT WHAT IF YOU AREN'T INTO
COLD CUTS ON TOP OF YOUR LETTUCE? THIS SALAD COMES TO THE RESCUE WITH A MIX OF CHICKPEAS AND AVOCADO,
WHICH PROVIDE PROTEIN, HEALTHY FAT AND PLEASING FLAVOURS.

METHOD

Pickle and Caper Dressing: In small bowl, stir together mayonnaise, dill pickle, oil, chili sauce, lemon juice, capers, mustard, salt and pepper.

In large bowl, toss together iceberg lettuce, radicchio, sprouts, radishes, cucumber, onion and half of the dressing; arrange on four large plates.

Top with chickpeas, eggs, tomato, avocado, and Swiss and Cheddar cheeses; spoon remaining dressing over top.

INGREDIENTS

6 cups	torn iceberg lettuce
2 cups	torn radicchio
½ cup	alfalfa sprouts (about half 35 g pkg)
4	radishes, thinly sliced
¾ cup	sliced English cucumber
⅓ cup	thinly sliced sweet onion
½ cup	rinsed drained canned chickpeas
3	hard-cooked eggs (see how-to, page 79), quartered
1	large tomato, cut in 12 wedges
Half	avocado, pitted, peeled and sliced
60 g	each Swiss and Cheddar cheeses, cut in sticks

Pickle and Caper Dressing:

¼ cup	light mayonnaise
1 tbsp	minced dill pickle
1 tbsp	extra-virgin olive oil
2 tsp	tomato-based chili sauce
1½ tsp	lemon juice
½ tsp	capers, drained and minced
½ tsp	Dijon mustard
Pinch	each salt and pepper

Makes 4 servings.

PER SERVING: about 349 cal, 16 g pro, 25 g total fat (9 g sat. fat), 17 g carb, 5 g fibre, 173 mg chol, 430 mg sodium. % RDI: 25% calcium, 14% iron, 20% vit A, 32% vit C, 60% folate.

FIG, PROSCIUTTO AND GORGONZOLA SALAD

THIS RECIPE MAKES DOUBLE THE DRESSING YOU NEED, BUT IT IS EXCELLENT ON OTHER SALADS AND KEEPS WELL IN THE REFRIGERATOR FOR UP TO FIVE DAYS. NOT A BLUE CHEESE FAN? SUBSTITUTE THE SAME AMOUNT OF SOFT GOAT CHEESE OR BRIE FOR THE GORGONZOLA.

INGREDIENTS

6	slices prosciutto (115 g)
12	dried Mission figs, halved (or 6 fresh figs, quartered)
12 cups	mixed baby greens (such as arugula, spinach, mâche and/or romaine)
115 g	Gorgonzola cheese, crumbled
¼ cup	sliced almonds, toasted (see tip, page 44)

Balsamic Dressing:

¼ cup	balsamic vinegar
2 tbsp	liquid honey
1 tsp	Dijon mustard
Pinch	each salt and pepper
⅓ cup	extra-virgin olive oil

METHOD

Balsamic Dressing: In small bowl, whisk together vinegar, honey, mustard, salt and pepper; slowly whisk in oil until emulsified.

Cut each prosciutto slice lengthwise into four strips; wrap each around one fig half. Arrange baby greens on serving platter; top with figs, then Gorgonzola cheese. Drizzle with half of the dressing, reserving remainder for another use. (*Make-ahead: Refrigerate dressing in airtight container for up to 5 days.*)

Sprinkle with almonds.

CHANGE IT UP

GRILLED FIG, PROSCIUTTO AND GORGONZOLA SALAD

Thread wrapped figs onto metal skewers. Place on greased grill over medium-high heat; close lid and grill, turning once, until prosciutto is slightly crisp, about 5 minutes.

Makes 4 servings.

PER SERVING: about 399 cal, 18 g pro, 26 g total fat (9 g sat. fat), 28 g carb, 5 g fibre, 57 mg chol, 1,184 mg sodium, 879 mg potassium. % RDI: 28% calcium, 25% iron, 94% vit A, 55% vit C, 59% folate.

LOBSTER, GREENS AND FENNEL
with creamy citrus dressing

A BRIGHT CITRUS DRESSING CUTS THE RICHNESS OF THE LOBSTER IN THIS COLOURFUL, ELEGANT SALAD.
IF YOU DON'T HAVE TIME TO FOLLOW OUR HOW-TO AND COOK THE LOBSTERS YOURSELF, ASK THE STAFF AT YOUR LOCAL
FISH COUNTER—THEY WILL OFTEN STEAM LOBSTERS TO ORDER, SAVING YOU THE WORK.

INGREDIENTS

2	cooked lobsters, each about 375 g (see how-to, below)
2	oranges
6 cups	lightly packed torn green leaf lettuce
1 cup	torn radicchio
1 cup	torn frisée
Half	bulb fennel, cored and thinly sliced

Creamy Citrus Dressing:

2 tbsp	extra-virgin olive oil
1 tbsp	chopped fresh chives
1 tbsp	lemon juice
1 tsp	mayonnaise
1 tsp	Dijon mustard
1	small shallot, minced
½ tsp	grated orange zest
Pinch	each salt and pepper

METHOD

Place each lobster on cutting board; twist off tail. With sharp chef's knife, cut tail in half lengthwise; remove meat from tail and cut into chunks. Place in large bowl.

Remove claws from body. With blunt side of knife, crack claws; pull shell apart and remove meat. Cut into chunks; add to bowl.

Working over separate bowl to catch juice, peel and segment oranges; set aside, reserving 1 tbsp of the juice.

Creamy Citrus Dressing: In glass measure, whisk together oil, chives, lemon juice, mayonnaise, mustard, shallot, orange zest, salt, pepper and reserved orange juice; set aside.

Add leaf lettuce, radicchio, frisée, fennel and orange sections to bowl with lobster. Drizzle dressing over top; toss to coat.

HOW TO
COOK FRESH LOBSTERS

Fill stockpot with enough salted water to completely cover lobsters; bring to full rolling boil over high heat. Plunge each lobster headfirst into water; cover and start timer when water returns to boil. Reduce heat and simmer until lobsters are bright red and small leg comes away easily when twisted and pulled, 8 to 10 minutes.

Makes 4 servings.

PER SERVING: about 169 cal, 11 g pro, 8 g total fat (1 g sat. fat), 14 g carb, 4 g fibre, 32 mg chol, 219 mg sodium, 634 mg potassium. % RDI: 11% calcium, 11% iron, 19% vit A, 90% vit C, 36% folate.

TROUT NIÇOISE SALAD

TUNA IS A TYPICAL TOPPER FOR A CLASSIC NIÇOISE, BUT FRESHLY COOKED TROUT GIVES THIS COMPOSED SALAD A NEW TWIST. SMALL PURPLISH-BLACK NIÇOISE OLIVES HAVE A NUTTY TASTE. IF YOU CAN'T FIND THEM, TRY KALAMATA OLIVES, WHICH ARE A COMMON OFFERING AT SUPERMARKET OLIVE BARS.

METHOD

In large pot of boiling lightly salted water, blanch green beans until tender-crisp, about 1 minute. Using tongs, transfer to bowl of ice water; let cool. Drain well.

Meanwhile, add potatoes to same pot of boiling water; cook until tender, about 12 minutes. Drain; cut in half.

Sprinkle fish with half each of the salt and pepper. In large skillet, heat ½ tsp of the oil over medium-high heat; cook trout, turning once, until fish flakes easily when tested, about 4 minutes.

Meanwhile, in small bowl, stir together lemon juice, tarragon, mustard, honey, and remaining salt and pepper; slowly whisk in remaining oil until emulsified.

Divide eggs, green beans, potatoes, baby greens, olives and tomatoes among four plates. Top each with one piece of the trout; drizzle with dressing.

INGREDIENTS

225 g	green beans, trimmed
10	mini yellow-fleshed potatoes
2	trout fillets (450 g total), halved crosswise
¼ tsp	each salt and pepper
⅓ cup	extra-virgin olive oil
¼ cup	lemon juice
2 tsp	finely chopped fresh tarragon
1 tsp	Dijon mustard
1 tsp	liquid honey
4	hard-cooked eggs (see how-to, page 79), halved lengthwise
4 cups	mixed baby greens
20	Niçoise or other black olives
2	small tomatoes, each cut in 6 wedges

Makes 4 servings.
PER SERVING: about 527 cal, 33 g pro, 35 g total fat (7 g sat. fat), 20 g carb, 3 g fibre, 251 mg chol, 690 mg sodium, 1,039 mg potassium. % RDI: 16% calcium, 17% iron, 34% vit A, 52% vit C, 55% folate.

ARUGULA SHRIMP SALAD

HOT PEPPER FLAKES GIVE THIS SHRIMP A SLIGHT HEAT THAT'S UNEXPECTED IN A SALAD.
THE COMBINATION OF ORANGE VINAIGRETTE, ORANGE SECTIONS AND CILANTRO GIVE
THE WHOLE DISH A SUNNY, BRIGHT FLAVOUR.

METHOD

Orange Vinaigrette: Grate enough orange zest to make 1 tsp; set aside. Working over large bowl, cut off rind and outer membrane of oranges; cut between membrane and pulp to release sections into bowl. Squeeze membranes to extract juice. Transfer 2 tbsp juice to small bowl; whisk in orange zest, oil, vinegar, salt and pepper. Set vinaigrette and orange sections aside.

In large skillet, heat oil over medium-high heat; sauté shrimp, garlic and hot pepper flakes until shrimp are pink and opaque, about 5 minutes. Add 2 tbsp of the vinaigrette; cook, stirring, until no liquid remains, about 3 minutes. Stir in cilantro.

Add arugula, croutons, onion and remaining vinaigrette to orange sections; toss to coat. Divide among four plates; top with shrimp and olives.

INGREDIENTS

1 tbsp	extra-virgin olive oil
450 g	raw medium shrimp, peeled and deveined
1	clove garlic, minced
¼ tsp	hot pepper flakes
3 tbsp	minced fresh cilantro or parsley
4 cups	arugula, trimmed
1 cup	croutons (such as Parmesan Croutons, page 66)
¼ cup	thinly sliced sweet onion
½ cup	green olives, pitted and halved

Orange Vinaigrette:

2	oranges
¼ cup	extra-virgin olive oil
2 tbsp	sherry vinegar
¼ tsp	each salt and pepper

Makes 4 servings.

PER SERVING: about 347 cal, 21 g pro, 22 g total fat (3 g sat. fat), 18 g carb, 3 g fibre, 129 mg chol, 624 mg sodium. % RDI: 16% calcium, 26% iron, 20% vit A, 77% vit C, 41% folate.

WHITE BEAN AND SMOKED SALMON SALAD

BREAD, BEANS AND SMOKED SALMON ARE ALL NATURALLY HIGH IN SODIUM, SO NO EXTRA SALT IS NEEDED IN THIS TASTY RECIPE. SMOKED TROUT MAKES A GREAT SUBSTITUTE FOR THE SALMON; IF YOU CAN'T FIND EITHER, A CAN OF SALMON OR TUNA WOULD BE TASTY, TOO.

INGREDIENTS

¼ cup	extra-virgin olive oil
Half	white onion, thinly sliced
2	ribs celery, thinly sliced
1	clove garlic, thinly sliced
1	can (540 mL) white kidney beans, drained and rinsed
1 tbsp	white wine vinegar
4 cups	loosely packed baby arugula
2 tbsp	each chopped fresh chives and parsley
150 g	hot-smoked salmon, broken in chunks

Peppery Garlic Croutons:

1 tbsp	extra-virgin olive oil
1	clove garlic, grated
¼ tsp	pepper
2 cups	cubed day-old crusty bread

METHOD

Peppery Garlic Croutons: In bowl, stir together oil, garlic and pepper; add bread cubes. Toss to coat. Bake on rimmed baking sheet in 350°F (180°C) oven, turning once, until crisp and golden, 10 to 12 minutes.

Meanwhile, in large skillet, heat oil over medium-high heat; cook onion, celery and garlic, stirring occasionally, until softened and light golden, about 6 minutes. Stir in beans and vinegar; cook, stirring, until heated through, about 2 minutes.

In large bowl, toss together warm bean mixture, arugula, chives and parsley; sprinkle with salmon and croutons.

Make a double or triple batch of the Peppery Garlic Croutons, and store them in an airtight container for up to 2 weeks. Use them to jazz up soups, salads and pasta dishes.

Makes 4 servings.

PER SERVING: about 368 cal, 17 g pro, 20 g total fat (3 g sat. fat), 32 g carb, 10 g fibre, 9 mg chol, 730 mg sodium, 656 mg potassium. % RDI: 15% calcium, 23% iron, 17% vit A, 22% vit C, 46% folate.

PORK TOSTADA SALAD

TOSTADAS ADD A CRUNCHY, SATISFYING DIMENSION TO THIS FUN MASHUP OF TACOS AND VEGGIES.
GROUND BEEF OR POULTRY ARE TASTY SUBSTITUTES FOR THE PORK IF YOU PREFER THEM.

METHOD

In large skillet, cook pork over medium-high heat, breaking up with spoon, until no longer pink, about 5 minutes.

Drain fat from pan; add chili powder, vinegar, salt, coriander, sugar, garlic and light green parts of green onions. Reduce heat to medium; cook, stirring often, for 5 minutes.

Place one tostada on each of four plates; top with about half each of the lettuce, tomato, pork mixture, salsa and Cheddar cheese. Repeat layers once, starting with tostada. Top with sour cream; sprinkle with dark green parts of green onions.

INGREDIENTS

450 g	lean ground pork
1 tbsp	chili powder
1 tbsp	wine vinegar
½ tsp	each salt and ground coriander
Pinch	granulated sugar
2	cloves garlic, minced
2	green onions, thinly sliced (light and dark green parts separated)
8	corn tostadas
2 cups	shredded iceberg or romaine lettuce
1	large tomato, chopped
½ cup	salsa
½ cup	shredded Cheddar cheese
¼ cup	light sour cream

TEST KITCHEN TIP

Tostadas are flat, crunchy taco shells that do not require heating. Look for them (plain or in flavoured varieties) in the Mexican section of the grocery store. If you can't find them, use tortilla chips instead.

PHOTO
PAGE 100

Makes 4 servings.

PER SERVING: about 422 cal, 28 g pro, 26 g total fat (10 g sat. fat), 21 g carb, 4 g fibre, 93 mg chol, 748 mg sodium. % RDI: 18% calcium, 16% iron, 16% vit A, 18% vit C, 17% folate.

PORK TOSTADA SALAD

PAGE 99

Edible Wild Spring Greens

Ever thought about harvesting what grows in your neighbourhood? Here's what to look for and how to do it safely.

FIDDLEHEADS
MATTEUCCIA STRUTHIOPTERIS

Ostrich ferns usually grow in clumps along swamp and river edges, and in the rich, moist soil in open woods or shady lowlands. The curled fronds of immature ferns are all called fiddleheads, but the ones we love to eat come from the ostrich fern.

Edibility: In early spring, look for bright green, tightly curled fronds covered in brown, papery scales on stalks 5 to 6 inches (12 to 15 cm) tall.

Preparation: Rub off scales and rinse well under cold running water. Use cooked: boil, blanch or sauté for at least 5 minutes.

WATERCRESS
NASTURTIUM OFFICINALE

Watercress grows in water or wet places. They have white roots and several pairs of small, dark green leaflets on stems ending with rounded larger leaves. Gather watercress only from uncontaminated locations.

Edibility: Gather leaves and stems from early spring to fall.

Preparation: Rinse well under cold running water. Use raw in salads, sauces and soufflés.

DANDELIONS
TARAXACUM OFFICINALE

The word *dandelion* comes from the French *dents de lion* (lion's teeth), for the sharp-toothed green leaves of this common weed. Fertilizers and herbicides used on lawns, roadsides and golf courses are not safe to ingest, so don't pick from an area unless you know its history.

Edibility: All parts of the plant are edible, but the leaves are best. Look for small, tender leaves of plants grown in shade; pick before blossoms appear for less bitter taste and the optimal texture. Dandelions contain large amounts of vitamin C.

Preparation: Trim off root ends. Rinse leaves well under cold running water and pat dry. Use raw in salads, or enjoy sautéed, braised or stir-fried.

FORAGING 101

All of the wild greens on this page are available on the shelves of grocery and specialty food stores, but it is very satisfying to seek out and pick (or forage) your own. Here are some guidelines to get you started.

- Purchase and follow an up-to-date, reputable field guide to edible wild plants. Start by learning to positively identify a few plants. If possible, go out with an expert at first.

- Do not gather anything unless you are 100 per cent sure of its identity.

- Pick precisely. Sometimes unpalatable or toxic plants can grow among the edible ones.

- Don't overharvest. Picking only some plants in an area leaves enough to harvest in following years. Alternate picking locations from year to year.

- Don't forage on private property, in areas where fertilizers or herbicides are sprayed, or near polluted waterways.

PORK AND NAPA SALAD

COOKED CABBAGE AND PORK ARE A MATCH MADE IN HEAVEN, ESPECIALLY IN ASIAN-INSPIRED DISHES LIKE THIS ONE. A MIX OF SESAME OIL, FISH SAUCE AND VINEGAR GIVES THE DRESSING A SAVOURY, TANGY FLAVOUR THAT REALLY COMPLEMENTS THE SWEET CABBAGE AND SPICED PORK.

METHOD

Stir together oil, garlic, salt, pepper, coriander and cloves; brush over pork. Let stand for 15 minutes.

Place pork on greased grill over medium-high heat; close lid and grill, turning three times, until juices run clear when pork is pierced and just a hint of pink remains inside, or instant-read thermometer inserted in thickest part reads 160°F (71°C), 15 to 20 minutes. Transfer to cutting board and tent with foil; let stand for 5 minutes before cutting into ½-inch (1 cm) thick slices.

Meanwhile, in bowl, combine cabbage, carrot, snap peas, green onions, lime juice, sesame oil, vinegar, fish sauce, sugar and ginger; toss to coat. Divide among four plates. Top with pork.

HOW TO

BLANCH AND REFRESH VEGETABLES OR FRUIT

Blanching means immersing an ingredient briefly in boiling water to partially cook it. Refreshing means dunking the blanched ingredient in ice water to quickly stop the cooking process. The quick chill (and a little added salt in the water, if you wish) helps veggies—especially green ones—maintain their vibrant colour. Using a 6:1 ratio of water to ingredient allows the water to return to a rapid boil as quickly as possible. The length of blanching depends on the ingredient and what purpose it will serve. For this salad, the snap peas only need 1 to 2 minutes of blanching to achieve just the right tender-crisp texture.

INGREDIENTS

1 tbsp	vegetable oil
2	cloves garlic, minced
½ tsp	each salt and pepper
½ tsp	ground coriander
¼ tsp	ground cloves
450 g	pork tenderloin
6 cups	shredded napa cabbage
1	carrot, julienned (see how-to, page 36)
1 cup	sugar snap peas, blanched (see how-to, below) and halved
2	green onions, thinly sliced
2 tbsp	lime juice
1 tbsp	sesame oil
1 tbsp	vinegar
1 tbsp	fish sauce
2 tsp	granulated sugar
2 tsp	minced fresh ginger

Makes 4 servings.

PER SERVING: about 247 cal, 28 g pro, 10 g total fat (2 g sat. fat), 13 g carb, 3 g fibre, 61 mg chol, 715 mg sodium. % RDI: 11% calcium, 16% iron, 31% vit A, 68% vit C, 53% folate.

JERK BEEF SALAD WITH GRILLED PEPPERS

A JAR OF JERK SEASONING IS HANDY TO KEEP IN THE FRIDGE FOR QUICK GRILLS. HERE, IT FLAVOURS A SIMPLE MARINADE FOR FLANK STEAK, A TOUGHER CUT OF BEEF USUALLY RESERVED FOR BRAISING. HOWEVER, WHEN IT'S BARBECUED BRIEFLY TO NO MORE THAN MEDIUM-RARE, THEN SLICED THINLY ACROSS THE GRAIN, FLANK STEAK IS TENDER AND JUICY.

INGREDIENTS

¼ cup	extra-virgin olive oil
4 tsp	lime juice
2 tsp	jerk seasoning
1 tsp	soy sauce
450 g	beef flank marinating steak
1	each sweet red, green and yellow pepper
1	small red onion
¼ tsp	each salt and pepper
8 cups	mixed greens

METHOD

In shallow bowl, whisk together 3 tbsp of the oil, lime juice, jerk seasoning and soy sauce. Remove 2 tbsp and set aside. Add steak to bowl and turn to coat. Let stand for 15 minutes. (*Make-ahead: Cover and refrigerate steak and reserved marinade separately for up to 8 hours.*)

Place steak on greased grill over medium heat; close lid and grill, turning once, until medium-rare, 10 to 12 minutes. Transfer to cutting board and tent with foil; let stand for 10 minutes before thinly slicing on angle across the grain.

Meanwhile, halve and seed sweet peppers; cut each half into three pieces. Cut onion into ½-inch (1 cm) thick slices. Brush peppers and onion with remaining oil; sprinkle with salt and pepper. Add to grill and cook, turning once, until softened, 12 to 15 minutes. Separate onion into rings.

In large bowl, toss greens with reserved marinade. Arrange on four plates; top with peppers, onion and steak.

Makes 4 servings.

PER SERVING: about 355 cal, 29 g pro, 23 g total fat (6 g sat. fat), 10 g carb, 3 g fibre, 46 mg chol, 509 mg sodium. % RDI: 8% calcium, 23% iron, 36% vit A, 218% vit C, 32% folate.

GRILLED STEAK AND POTATO SALAD

DOES YOUR FAMILY LOVE MEAT AND POTATOES, BUT YOU WANT THEM TO EAT
MORE VEGETABLES? HERE'S THE ULTIMATE COMPROMISE: ALL THE PLEASURE OF
GRILLED STEAK AND POTATOES MIXED INTO A TASTY, FRESH SUMMER SALAD.

INGREDIENTS

2 tbsp	olive oil
1 tsp	each sweet paprika and dried oregano
¼ tsp	each salt and pepper
450 g	mini red-skinned potatoes (about 16)
450 g	beef flank marinating steak
8 cups	lightly packed mixed baby greens
1 cup	thinly sliced cored fennel bulb
1 cup	halved grape tomatoes
¼ cup	crumbled blue cheese

Easy Dijon Vinaigrette:

2 tbsp	extra-virgin olive oil
1 tbsp	wine vinegar
1 tsp	Dijon mustard
Pinch	each salt and pepper

METHOD

Stir together oil, paprika, oregano, salt and pepper; set aside.

Scrub and halve potatoes. Place in microwaveable dish; sprinkle with 2 tbsp water. Cover and microwave on high until tender, 5 to 8 minutes. Toss with half of the paprika mixture; thread onto metal or soaked wooden skewers.

Rub remaining paprika mixture all over steak. Place steak and potatoes on greased grill over medium-high heat; close lid and grill, turning once, until steak is medium-rare and potatoes are tender, 10 to 12 minutes.

Transfer steak to cutting board; let stand for 5 minutes before thinly slicing across the grain. Remove potatoes from skewers.

Easy Dijon Vinaigrette: Meanwhile, in large bowl, whisk together oil, vinegar, mustard, salt and pepper.

Add baby greens, fennel, tomatoes, potatoes and steak to vinaigrette; toss to coat. Sprinkle with blue cheese.

Makes 4 servings.
PER SERVING: about 428 cal, 30 g pro, 23 g total fat (6 g sat. fat), 25 g carb, 5 g fibre, 55 mg chol, 366 mg sodium, 1,231 mg potassium. % RDI: 14% calcium, 31% iron, 31% vit A, 67% vit C, 58% folate.

Tools of the Salad Trade

To be fair, salads are pretty easy to make without a lot of special equipment.
But here are a few tools that might make the job more efficient and pleasant.

SALAD SPINNER

This bulky gadget may take up a lot of cupboard space, but it makes washing and prepping greens and herbs a lot easier. Look for a large-capacity bowl so greens have plenty of room to move and you have fewer batches to spin. There are lots of different spinning mechanisms—cranks, buttons, pull cords and more—so try before you buy, and see how much force is necessary to get (and keep) the basket insert whirling. Also check for a sturdy, nonskid base that will keep the bowl from zipping across the counter if you let go. A brake to stop the spin is handy. Some have bowls that conveniently double as a salad bowls.

FANCY SLICERS

Slicing isn't tough if you have a sharp knife and a good cutting board, but there are a couple of gadgets that promise to make even this simple task simpler. Check your local kitchenware store for avocado slicers, egg slicers, multibladed rolling herb choppers and many more.

TONGS

Sure, an old-fashioned set of salad spoons looks great, but a good pair of tongs makes serving a breeze. Plain metal chef's tongs work well but aren't much to look at on the table. Hinged salad tongs don't slip and make serving a one-handed operation. You may also want to look for some funky "salad hands," which grab big handfuls without making a mess.

MANDOLINE

A mandoline is just the tool for efficient, even slicing. Fancy models come with a variety of blades, such as julienne, thick and thin slice, crinkle-cut and even waffle-cut. Mandoline blades are seriously sharp, like razors, so use great care when handling them. A studded handle comes with most; use it to hold the food against the blade and protect your fingers. If you use the mandoline without it, you risk a nasty cut. The slicer blade on your food processor can stand in for a mandoline if you don't have space for another kitchen gadget.

VEGETABLE PEELER

A sharp vegetable peeler works well for a variety of salad-making tasks, from peeling a carrot to shaving delicate shreds of Parmesan cheese off a wedge. It's up to you whether you prefer the Y-shaped handle or the straight swivel-blade variety. Fancier versions have blades that do all sorts of interesting tasks, including julienning and peeling skin off delicate ingredients, such as tomatoes or mangoes.

GRATER

There are many types of this must-have kitchen tool. Start with an old-fashioned box grater, which can slice, grate and shred (just watch your fingers!). Then add a rasp grater, which is terrific for zesting citrus fruits and grating ginger or garlic for dressings. And if you have a food processor or stand mixer, check to see if you have a shredder blade attachment. It makes surprisingly short work of shredding cabbage for slaws.

GRILLED STEAK AND ASPARAGUS SALAD

IT'S EASY TO GRILL THE ULTIMATE STEAK: JUST PREHEAT THE GRILL, AND DON'T TOUCH THE MEAT TOO MUCH AS IT COOKS. LET THE STEAK REST BEFORE SLICING IT SO THE JUICES REDISTRIBUTE; THE MEAT WILL BE PERFECTLY JUICY WHEN CUT.

METHOD

Combine celery seeds, salt, pepper and garlic powder; rub all over steak. Brush onion with some of the oil; toss asparagus with remaining oil.

Place steak, onion and asparagus on greased grill over medium-high heat; close lid and grill, turning once, until steak is medium-rare, onion is softened and asparagus is tender-crisp, about 8 minutes. Transfer to cutting board; let steak stand for 5 minutes before thinly slicing. Meanwhile, halve onion rings and asparagus.

Pesto Vinaigrette: Meanwhile, in large bowl, whisk together oil, vinegar, pesto and pepper. Add lettuce, onion and asparagus; toss to coat. Sprinkle with goat cheese; top with steak.

INGREDIENTS

½ tsp	celery seeds
¼ tsp	each salt and pepper
¼ tsp	garlic powder
450 g	beef strip loin grilling steak (1 inch/2.5 cm thick)
1	red onion, cut in ½-inch (1 cm) thick rings
2 tsp	olive oil
1	bunch (450 g) asparagus, trimmed (see how-to, page 175)
6 cups	torn romaine lettuce hearts
70 g	pepper-crusted goat cheese, crumbled

Pesto Vinaigrette:

¼ cup	extra-virgin olive oil
3 tbsp	balsamic vinegar
2 tbsp	sun-dried tomato pesto
¼ tsp	pepper

Makes 4 servings.

PER SERVING: about 427 cal, 33 g pro, 26 g total fat (8 g sat. fat), 15 g carb, 4 g fibre, 64 mg chol, 339 mg sodium, 685 mg potassium. % RDI: 8% calcium, 32% iron, 57% vit A, 38% vit C, 92% folate.

STEAK SALAD
with tangy blue cheese dressing

THIS SIMPLE BLUE CHEESE DRESSING IS JUST THE TICKET TO GO WITH TENDER GRILLED STRIP LOIN STEAK AND SALAD. IT'S ALSO A QUICK AND TASTY DIP FOR HOMEMADE WINGS.

INGREDIENTS

450 g	beef strip loin grilling steak, about 1 inch (2.5 cm) thick
½ tsp	each salt and pepper
1	head Boston or Bibb lettuce, torn
½ cup	thinly sliced radishes
½ cup	cherry tomatoes, halved
1	avocado, pitted, peeled and sliced
2	green onions, chopped

Tangy Blue Cheese Dressing:

⅓ cup	buttermilk
¼ cup	crumbled blue cheese
3 tbsp	light mayonnaise
1 tsp	white wine vinegar
1 tsp	Dijon mustard

METHOD

Tangy Blue Cheese Dressing: In food processor, purée together buttermilk, blue cheese, mayonnaise, vinegar and mustard until smooth. Set aside.

Sprinkle steak with salt and pepper. Place on greased grill or in grill pan over medium-high heat; close lid and grill, turning once, until medium-rare, about 8 minutes. Transfer to cutting board and tent with foil; let stand for 10 minutes before thinly slicing across the grain.

Meanwhile, divide lettuce, radishes, tomatoes and avocado among four plates. Top with steak and blue cheese dressing; sprinkle with green onions.

Makes 4 servings.

PER SERVING: about 369 cal, 26 g pro, 27 g total fat (9 g sat. fat), 9 g carb, 5 g fibre, 72 mg chol, 576 mg sodium, 795 mg potassium. % RDI: 11% calcium, 18% iron, 9% vit A, 26% vit C, 42% folate.

112

BEAN & GRAIN

RECIPES

QUINOA AND CHICKPEA SALAD
with tomato vinaigrette

QUINOA IS SO POPULAR RIGHT NOW, YOU SEE IT EVERYWHERE. IT'S A HEALTHY, GLUTEN-FREE WHOLE GRAIN, AND IT SOAKS UP SAUCES AND VINAIGRETTES BEAUTIFULLY—PERFECT FOR A PORTABLE SALAD LIKE THIS. IT MAKES A DELIGHTFUL LUNCH OR POTLUCK DISH.

INGREDIENTS

1 cup	quinoa, rinsed and drained (see how-to, page 141)
2 cups	green beans, trimmed and chopped
1	can (540 mL) chickpeas, drained and rinsed
1	sweet red pepper, diced
1 cup	crumbled feta cheese

Tomato Vinaigrette:

⅓ cup	bottled strained tomatoes (passata)
3 tbsp	red wine vinegar
3 tbsp	olive oil
3 tbsp	liquid honey
½ tsp	dried Italian herb seasoning
½ tsp	salt
¼ tsp	pepper
Pinch	cayenne pepper

METHOD

In saucepan, bring quinoa and 2 cups water to boil; reduce heat, cover and simmer for 12 minutes. Fluff with fork; let cool.

Meanwhile, in saucepan of boiling salted water, blanch green beans until tender-crisp, about 3 minutes. Using tongs, transfer to bowl of ice water; let cool. Drain well; transfer to large bowl. Stir in cooled quinoa, chickpeas, red pepper and feta cheese.

Tomato Vinaigrette: Whisk together strained tomatoes, vinegar, oil, honey, Italian herb seasoning, salt, pepper and cayenne pepper; pour over quinoa mixture. Stir to coat.

Makes 4 servings.

PER SERVING: about 556 cal, 18 g pro, 22 g total fat (8 g sat. fat), 75 g carb, 9 g fibre, 35 mg chol, 1,155 mg sodium, 649 mg potassium. % RDI: 25% calcium, 46% iron, 18% vit A, 108% vit C, 53% folate.

Cooking Dried Beans

Dried beans are not as convenient as ready-to-eat canned beans, but they're lower in sodium and cost less. Here are some guidelines that make it easy to include these nutritious, money-saving legumes in your diet.

SOAKING

- Most dried legumes (or beans)—except lentils and split peas—need to be soaked before cooking. First, put the beans in a colander and pick through them to remove any small stones, and any wrinkled or discoloured beans. Rinse the beans well under cold water. Drain.

  - **Overnight-soak method:** Combine beans with three times their volume of water. Cover and soak them overnight at room temperature. Drain.
  - **Quick-soak method:** In large saucepan, combine beans with three times their volume of water. Bring to boil; boil gently for 2 minutes. Remove from heat, cover and let stand for 1 hour. Drain.

- In saucepan, cover soaked beans (either method) again with three times their volume of water and bring to boil. Reduce heat, cover and simmer until tender, 30 to 80 minutes depending on bean variety (see Cooking Times, right). Reserving cooking liquid to use in recipe, drain.

- To calculate yields, 1 cup dried beans generally simmers into about 2 cups cooked beans, but some varieties can yield up to ½ cup more.

COOKING TIMES

- Cooking times vary among dried beans. The soaking method also changes the cooking time: Count on 5 to 10 minutes less time if you're using the quick-soak method.

- Start checking the beans, regardless of the soaking method, by tasting them about 10 minutes before the suggested cooking time is done. Check every 5 minutes thereafter. A well-cooked bean is tender and easy to squash in your mouth.

  - **Black beans:** 30 minutes
  - **Black-eyed peas:** 35 minutes
  - **Chickpeas:** 45 minutes
  - **Kidney beans (white and red):** 50 minutes
  - **Large lima beans:** 55 minutes
  - **Navy beans:** 40 minutes
  - **Romano beans:** 45 minutes

WARM BLACK-EYED PEA AND FENNEL SALAD

THE WARM PEAS DELICIOUSLY ABSORB THE DRESSING IN THIS VEGGIE AND BEAN COMBO.
TO KEEP THE SALAD MOIST, DRIZZLE WITH ADDITIONAL OIL AND VINEGAR JUST BEFORE SERVING.

METHOD

In shallow Dutch oven or skillet, heat 3 tbsp of the oil over medium heat; cook fennel, celery, garlic, thyme and salt, stirring occasionally, until softened and beginning to colour, about 8 minutes.

Stir in 1 tbsp of the vinegar, the black-eyed peas and parsley; cook for 2 minutes. Transfer to serving bowl; toss with remaining oil and vinegar, adding more if desired. Serve warm.

INGREDIENTS

¼ cup	extra-virgin olive oil (approx)
1 cup	thinly sliced cored fennel bulb (about half bulb)
½ cup	thinly sliced celery
3	cloves garlic, minced
½ tsp	each dried thyme and salt
4 tsp	white wine vinegar (approx)
3 cups	cooked black-eyed peas (see Cooking Dried Beans, opposite)
¼ cup	chopped fresh parsley

Makes 6 to 8 servings.

PER EACH OF 8 SERVINGS: about 142 cal, 5 g pro, 7 g total fat (1 g sat. fat), 15 g carb, 5 g fibre, 0 mg chol, 159 mg sodium. % RDI: 3% calcium, 14% iron, 2% vit A, 7% vit C, 64% folate.

MARINATED CHICKPEA SALAD

CANNED CHICKPEAS ARE A CONVENIENT SHORTCUT FOR MAKING THIS MARINATED SALAD.
IF YOU PREFER TO USE DRIED ONES INSTEAD, TURN TO PAGE 116 FOR OUR HOW-TO GUIDE. LEMON JUICE
ADDS BRIGHT FLAVOUR AND MELLOWS OUT THE RAW ONION.

INGREDIENTS

3 tbsp	lemon juice
2 tbsp	olive oil
¾ tsp	ground coriander
¼ tsp	pepper
Pinch	cayenne pepper
Pinch	salt
1	can (540 mL) chickpeas, drained and rinsed
1	baby cucumber, quartered lengthwise and sliced
⅓ cup	diced red onion
¼ cup	chopped fresh cilantro

METHOD

In bowl, whisk together lemon juice, oil, coriander, pepper, cayenne pepper and salt.

Add chickpeas, cucumber and onion; stir to combine. Cover and refrigerate for 2 hours. (*Make-ahead: Refrigerate for up to 24 hours.*)

Stir in chopped cilantro.

HOW TO

WASH CILANTRO AND KEEP IT FRESH

Cilantro is often gritty, so it requires a good rinse before use in recipes. Wash and store it the same way you would greens (for instructions, turn to page 24). When a bunch is clean and ready in the crisper, you're more likely to use up every last bit. Cilantro also browns and wilts easily, especially when it's kept uncovered in a cold refrigerator or chopped and left to stand for too long. Chop it at the last moment and add to dishes just before serving for the best flavour and brightest colour.

Makes 4 servings.
PER SERVING: about 199 cal, 6 g pro, 8 g total fat (1 g sat. fat), 27 g carb, 5 g fibre, 0 mg chol, 279 mg sodium, 226 mg potassium. % RDI: 4% calcium, 11% iron, 1% vit A, 17% vit C, 31% folate.

CURRIED LENTIL, WILD RICE AND ORZO SALAD

THIS INNOVATIVE, COOL SALAD HAS A LITTLE OF EVERYTHING—CHEWY BROWN RICE, EARTHY LENTILS AND TENDER ORZO. IT PARTNERS WELL WITH ANY MAIN DISH AND IS REALLY NICE WITH GRILLED OR ROASTED MEATS.

INGREDIENTS

½ cup	wild rice
⅔ cup	dried green or brown lentils
½ cup	orzo pasta
½ cup	dried currants
¼ cup	finely chopped red onion
⅓ cup	slivered almonds, toasted (see tip, page 44)

Curry Dressing:

¼ cup	white wine vinegar
1 tsp	ground cumin
1 tsp	Dijon mustard
½ tsp	each granulated sugar and salt
½ tsp	ground coriander
¼ tsp	each turmeric, sweet paprika and nutmeg
Pinch	each cinnamon, ground cloves and cayenne pepper
⅓ cup	canola or vegetable oil

METHOD

In large pot of boiling salted water, cover and cook wild rice for 10 minutes.

Add lentils; cook for 20 minutes. Add orzo; cook just until tender, about 5 minutes. Drain well; transfer to large bowl. Add currants and red onion.

Curry Dressing: In small bowl, whisk together vinegar, cumin, mustard, sugar, salt, coriander, turmeric, paprika, nutmeg, cinnamon, cloves and cayenne pepper; whisk in oil.

Pour dressing over wild rice mixture; gently toss to coat. Let cool. Cover and refrigerate until chilled, about 4 hours. *(Make-ahead: Refrigerate for up to 24 hours.)*

Serve sprinkled with almonds.

Lentils are no-soak legumes and come in lots of colours. They're a staple protein in many parts of the world. In North America, dried red, brown and green lentils are the most common. Red lentils are the smallest; their mild flavour is terrific in stews, soups and dips, but they don't hold their shape well enough to work in salads. Brown lentils are the most common and have a spicy, earthy flavour that's excellent in salads, soups and stews. Smaller green lentils have a rich flavour and hold their shape very well when cooked (slightly better than brown lentils), making them ideal in salads.

Makes 12 servings.

PER SERVING: about 178 cal, 6 g pro, 8 g total fat (1 g sat. fat), 22 g carb, 3 g fibre, 0 mg chol, 178 mg sodium, 231 mg potassium. % RDI: 2% calcium, 13% iron, 2% vit C, 30% folate.

GREEN BEAN AND BARLEY SALAD

THIS UNUSUAL MIXTURE OF CRUNCHY, FRESH BEANS AND CHEWY, HEARTY BARLEY
MAKES A TASTY COMBINATION. THIS SALAD CAN BE MADE AHEAD, SO IT'S PERFECT FOR A PICNIC OR
A NUTRITIOUS PACKED LUNCH TO TAKE TO SCHOOL OR WORK.

METHOD

Trim beans; halve diagonally. In saucepan of boiling water, blanch beans until tender-crisp, about 3 minutes. Using tongs, transfer to bowl of ice water; let cool. Drain well; pat dry.

Meanwhile, in pot of boiling salted water, cook barley until tender, 20 to 25 minutes. Drain; let cool for 5 minutes.

In large bowl, whisk together oil, vinegar, garlic, thyme, mustard, salt and pepper; add barley and green beans. Toss to coat.

Add arugula, tomatoes and green onions; toss well. (Make-ahead: Cover and let stand for up to 1 hour or refrigerate for up to 4 hours.) Stir in feta cheese.

INGREDIENTS

450 g	green beans
1 cup	pot or pearl barley
¼ cup	extra-virgin olive oil
3 tbsp	white wine vinegar
1	clove garlic, minced
1½ tsp	minced fresh thyme
1½ tsp	Dijon mustard
½ tsp	salt
¼ tsp	pepper
4 cups	baby arugula
2 cups	grape or cherry tomatoes, halved
2	green onions, thinly sliced
⅔ cup	crumbled feta cheese (about 100 g)

Makes 12 servings.

PER SERVING: about 142 cal, 4 g pro, 7 g total fat (2 g sat. fat), 18 g carb, 3 g fibre, 8 mg chol, 254 mg sodium, 231 mg potassium. % RDI: 9% calcium, 9% iron, 10% vit A, 17% vit C, 20% folate.

HONEY-LIME OAT AND BLACK BEAN SALAD

OATS AREN'T JUST FOR COOKIES OR PORRIDGE ANYMORE. OAT GROATS ARE SIMPLY CLEANED, TOASTED AND HULLED WHOLE OATS; BECAUSE THEY ARE MINIMALLY PROCESSED, THEY RETAIN MUCH OF THEIR NUTRITIOUS BRAN, GERM AND ENDOSPERM. THEY MAKE A NICE CHANGE FROM OTHER, MORE FAMILIAR SALAD GRAINS.

METHOD

In large saucepan, bring 2 cups water to boil; add oat groats. Reduce heat and simmer, uncovered and stirring occasionally, until tender and no liquid remains, about 45 minutes. Drain and rinse under cold water; drain again.

Honey-Lime Vinaigrette: Meanwhile, whisk together oil, lime zest, lime juice, honey, chili powder, salt and pepper.

In large bowl, combine oat groats, beans, tomatoes, jalapeño pepper and onion. Add vinaigrette; toss to coat. Cover and refrigerate for 1 hour. *(Make-ahead: Refrigerate in airtight container for up to 24 hours.)*

Just before serving, stir in avocado; sprinkle with cilantro.

CHANGE IT UP
HONEY-LIME WHOLE GRAIN AND BLACK BEAN SALAD

Substitute any whole grain, such as wheat berries, whole spelt or brown rice, for the oat groats, cooking according to package directions.

INGREDIENTS

1 cup	oat groats
1 cup	rinsed drained canned black beans
1 cup	halved cherry tomatoes
1	jalapeño pepper, seeded and finely chopped
2 tbsp	finely chopped red onion
Half	ripe avocado, pitted, peeled and diced
1 tbsp	chopped fresh cilantro

Honey-Lime Vinaigrette:

3 tbsp	vegetable oil
1 tsp	grated lime zest
3 tbsp	lime juice
1 tbsp	liquid honey
¼ tsp	chili powder
¼ tsp	each salt and pepper

Makes 6 servings.
PER SERVING: about 241 cal, 7 g pro, 11 g total fat (1 g sat. fat), 30 g carb, 6 g fibre, 0 mg chol, 205 mg sodium, 368 mg potassium. % RDI: 3% calcium, 14% iron, 3% vit A, 17% vit C, 17% folate.

GLUTEN-FREE QUINOA SALAD
with creamy tahini dressing

THE AMOUNT OF WATER YOU NEED TO COOK QUINOA VARIES, SO CHECK THE PACKAGE INSTRUCTIONS FOR BEST RESULTS. FOR A NUTTY TWIST, TOP THE SALAD WITH TOASTED SLIVERED ALMONDS (SEE TIP, PAGE 44).

INGREDIENTS

1 cup	quinoa, rinsed and drained (see how-to, page 141)
¼ tsp	salt
2 cups	grape or cherry tomatoes, halved
1 cup	diced English cucumber
1 cup	rinsed drained canned lentils
⅔ cup	chopped fresh parsley
⅓ cup	chopped fresh mint
3	green onions, thinly sliced

Creamy Tahini Dressing:

¼ cup	lemon juice
¼ cup	extra-virgin olive oil
¼ cup	warm water
¼ cup	tahini
1	small clove garlic, minced
½ tsp	ground cumin
¼ tsp	pepper
¼ tsp	salt

METHOD

In saucepan, bring 2 cups water, quinoa and salt to boil over high heat; reduce heat, cover and simmer until no liquid remains and quinoa is tender, about 15 minutes. Let cool.

Creamy Tahini Dressing: In large bowl, whisk together lemon juice, oil, warm water, tahini, garlic, cumin, pepper and salt.

Add quinoa, tomatoes, cucumber, lentils, parsley, mint and green onions to dressing; toss to coat. (*Make-ahead: Cover and refrigerate for up to 3 days.*)

Many recipes call for only small amounts of tahini. So what do you do with the rest of that huge jar? Technically, tahini doesn't need to be refrigerated and will keep at room temperature for many months, but keeping it in the fridge can stave off spoilage even a bit longer. Use it lavishly in homemade hummus, baba ghanoush and dips, or add a spoonful to your morning smoothie to give it a healthy nutrient boost and a creamy texture.

Makes 4 to 6 servings.
PER EACH OF 6 SERVINGS: about 300 cal, 9 g pro, 16 g total fat (2 g sat. fat), 32 g carb, 6 g fibre, 0 mg chol, 291 mg sodium, 581 mg potassium. % RDI: 9% calcium, 43% iron, 12% vit A, 33% vit C, 48% folate.

Perfect Salad Grains

Quinoa may be familiar, but there are a lot of options for making grain salads these days.
Here are some superstars you might want to add to your pantry.

BARLEY

Available in whole grain (pot barley) and refined (pearl barley) forms, this ancient grain is a staple for risottos, soups and salads. Whole grain barley is high in fibre, including beta-glucan, a soluble fibre also found in oats that helps lower bad cholesterol. Pearl barley has the bran and germ removed, so it's less nutritious but has a lovely, tender texture when cooked.

OATS

Rolled flakes are the most familiar form of this grain, used to make oatmeal and in baking. For salads, oat groats are the star. These unprocessed berries (or kernels) of the plant are whole grains, packed with soluble and insoluble fibre. The soluble fibre lowers cholesterol and helps keep blood sugar steady, making it excellent for people with diabetes. Groats are tender with a firm bite when cooked, and they're great at soaking up vinaigrettes. If the package is labelled "pure uncontaminated oats," they are gluten-free as well.

QUINOA

An ancient staple in South America, quinoa is the seed of a grass (not grain) plant, which means it's gluten-free. It offers protein along with carbohydrates and is a source of iron, zinc and folate. You'll find both red and white quinoa in stores, and both are equally nutritious. It's wonderful in grain salads, stuffings and side dishes.

RICE

White and brown rice come from the same plant; brown rice is the whole grain that contains the bran and the germ, while white rice has had both polished off. Both are great at absorbing dressings in salads. Brown rice is much higher in fibre, vitamins and minerals than white rice, and it offers a chewier texture and nuttier flavour that make salads taste more substantial. Fragrant white rice, such as basmati and jasmine, are especially tasty options.

RYE

Whole grain rye is high in fibre and contains a bunch of good-for-you vitamins and minerals. The unrefined berries (or kernels) are tasty in grain salads and can be substituted for wheat berries in many recipes. They have a stronger, earthier flavour than wheat berries.

WHEAT

Wheat flour is used to make couscous, a North African pasta that's a staple in many grain salads. There are white and whole wheat versions; both are ready after just a quick soak in boiling water, making them a great solution for busy nights. Whole wheat berries are unrefined and packed with fibre and nutrients; they make nice salads thanks to their pleasantly chewy texture. Spelt or kamut berries, two older forms of wheat, are tasty substitutes. Bulgur, a parboiled form of wheat, is another staple for grain salads. It's best known as the main ingredient in Middle Eastern tabbouleh.

WILD RICE

This "grain" is actually a seed from an aquatic grass that's native to Canada. It's a nutritious option for people following a gluten-free diet. The kernels have a chewy texture and a nutty, slightly smoky flavour when cooked. Wild rice can be pricey, but a little goes a long way, adding texture and flavour to salads, side dishes and stuffings.

WHEAT BERRY, CORN AND RED PEPPER SALAD

A WHEAT BERRY IS JUST THE INTACT, UNPROCESSED WHOLE GRAIN OF WHEAT. IT HAS LOTS OF FIBRE AND VITAMINS, SO IT'S AN EXCELLENT ADDITION TO YOUR DIET. HERE IT'S PAIRED WITH SWEET CORN AND RED PEPPERS FOR A NUTRITIOUS, SCRUMPTIOUS ONE-DISH MEAL.

METHOD

Smoked Paprika Vinaigrette: In large bowl, whisk together vinegar, garlic, mustard, paprika, salt and pepper; slowly whisk in oil until emulsified. Set aside.

In saucepan of boiling salted water, cook wheat berries until tender, about 1 hour. Add corn; cook for 30 seconds. Drain and rinse under cold water; drain again. Add to vinaigrette.

Add red pepper, green onions and basil; toss to combine. Cover and refrigerate for 1 hour before serving. (*Make-ahead: Refrigerate in airtight container for up to 24 hours.*)

INGREDIENTS

1 cup	wheat berries
1 cup	frozen corn kernels
1	sweet red pepper, diced
4	green onions, sliced
5	leaves fresh basil, shredded (see how-to, page 254)

Smoked Paprika Vinaigrette:

3 tbsp	white wine vinegar
1	clove garlic, minced
1 tsp	Dijon mustard
½ tsp	smoked paprika
¼ tsp	each salt and pepper
3 tbsp	vegetable oil

Makes 8 servings.

PER SERVING: about 149 cal, 4 g pro, 6 g total fat (1 g sat. fat), 23 g carb, 4 g fibre, 0 mg chol, 506 mg sodium, 188 mg potassium. % RDI: 2% calcium, 8% iron, 7% vit A, 43% vit C, 9% folate.

THREE-BEAN SALAD

THIS SALAD BAR CLASSIC IS SO MUCH BETTER WHEN MADE FRESH AT HOME. TRY IT WITH YELLOW BEANS WHEN THEY'RE IN SEASON—LOOK FOR THEM AT FARMER'S MARKETS ANYTIME BETWEEN JULY AND SEPTEMBER, WHEN THEY'RE AT THEIR PEAK.

128

INGREDIENTS

1½ cups	cut (2 inches/5 cm) green and/or yellow beans
¼ cup	extra-virgin olive oil
¼ cup	wine vinegar
1	clove garlic, minced
2 tbsp	chopped fresh parsley
½ tsp	granulated sugar
½ tsp	salt
¼ tsp	dried oregano
¼ tsp	pepper
1	can (540 mL) chickpeas, drained and rinsed
1	can (540 mL) red kidney beans, drained and rinsed
2	green onions, thinly sliced

METHOD

In saucepan of boiling salted water, blanch green beans until tender-crisp, 3 to 5 minutes. Using tongs, transfer to bowl of ice water; let cool. Drain well; shake off water. Place on tea towel; pat dry. Set aside.

In large bowl, whisk together oil, vinegar, garlic, parsley, sugar, salt, oregano and pepper.

Add chickpeas, kidney beans, green onions and green beans; toss to coat. (*Make-ahead: Cover and refrigerate for up to 8 hours.*)

Makes 6 to 8 servings.
PER EACH OF 8 SERVINGS: about 197 cal, 7 g pro, 8 g total fat (1 g sat. fat), 26 g carb, 8 g fibre, 0 mg chol, 505 mg sodium. % RDI: 4% calcium, 13% iron, 2% vit A, 10% vit C, 33% folate.

TABBOULEH

BULGUR IS CHEWY AND GREAT AT SOAKING UP DRESSINGS. IT'S THE STAR IN THIS BELOVED SALAD, WHICH IS A STAPLE ON MIDDLE EASTERN TABLES. FULL OF JUICY TOMATOES AND FRESH HERBS, IT'S LOVELY WITH GRILLED MEATS AND MAKES A REFRESHING TOPPING FOR PITA SANDWICHES, SUCH AS FALAFEL.

METHOD

Place bulgur in fine sieve; rinse several times with water. Transfer to bowl; cover with ½ inch (1 cm) water. Let stand for 20 minutes. Drain; one handful at a time, squeeze out excess water.

In large bowl, combine bulgur, tomatoes, parsley, mint and green onions. Whisk together lemon juice, oil, salt and pepper; add to bulgur mixture. Toss to coat. (Make-ahead: Cover and set aside for up to 8 hours.)

INGREDIENTS

½ cup	medium bulgur
3 cups	chopped seeded tomatoes
1 cup	minced fresh parsley
¼ cup	minced fresh mint
4	green onions, minced
½ cup	lemon juice
¼ cup	extra-virgin olive oil
¼ tsp	each salt and pepper

TEST KITCHEN TIP

Bulgur is ground to different coarseness levels: fine, medium and coarse are the most common, but some producers also create an extra-coarse grind for use in pilafs and very hearty soups. Fine bulgur is great for cooking tender baked goods and desserts, and some people prefer it to make more delicately textured grain salads. Medium bulgur is the all-purpose grind that's the star of tabbouleh and other salads, pilafs, soups and patties. It's also the main ingredient in the popular Lebanese dish kibbeh (or kibbe), which are fried bulgur croquettes stuffed with meat. Coarse bulgur is best suited for use in stuffings and heartier fare. Medium bulgur is easy to find in most supermarkets; look for all coarseness levels in Middle Eastern grocery stores.

Makes 4 servings.

PER SERVING: about 223 cal, 4 g pro, 14 g total fat (2 g sat. fat), 23 g carb, 6 g fibre, 0 mg chol, 178 mg sodium. % RDI: 6% calcium, 20% iron, 28% vit A, 82% vit C, 30% folate.

LENTIL AND SWEET POTATO SALAD

BABY ARUGULA GIVES THIS DISH A FRESHER, GREENER TASTE THAN OTHER LENTIL SALADS. SERVE IT AS
A LIGHT LUNCH OR A SIDE DISH WITH YOUR FAVOURITE GRILLED CHICKEN RECIPE.

130

INGREDIENTS

½ cup	dried green lentils
1	sweet potato, peeled and cubed
3 tbsp	extra-virgin olive oil
2 tbsp	balsamic vinegar
¼ tsp	each salt and pepper
1 cup	baby arugula
¼ cup	crumbled soft goat cheese

METHOD

In large saucepan of boiling water, cook lentils until tender, about 25 minutes. Drain.

Meanwhile, toss sweet potato with 1 tsp of the oil. Roast on baking sheet in 400°F (200°C) oven, turning once, until golden and tender, about 15 minutes.

In bowl, whisk together balsamic vinegar, remaining oil, salt and pepper; add lentils, sweet potato and arugula. Toss to coat; top with goat cheese.

TEST KITCHEN TIP

This recipe doubles just fine to feed more people. A double batch of the roasted sweet potato alone makes a yummy side dish; it's a simpler (and healthier) version of sweet potato fries.

Makes 2 servings.

PER SERVING: about 554 cal, 19 g pro, 25 g total fat (5 g sat. fat), 67 g carb, 11 g fibre, 8 mg chol, 413 mg sodium, 1,032 mg potassium. % RDI: 11% calcium, 49% iron, 319% vit A, 48% vit C, 125% folate.

Pack a Salad for Lunch

Sick of sandwiches? Try fresh salads this week for a change of pace, plus a nutritious vitamin and mineral boost. These tips make it easy.

STOCK UP

- If you're a newbie to making creative salads, choose some recipes that inspire you and start with those. Try something familiar at first, then branch out with new ideas, new flavours and new textures.

- Make a list before you shop. It's easy to get overwhelmed and head home with all the same staples. It's equally easy to get too inspired and find yourself with way more vegetables than you can use in a week. A list will keep you focused on what you need.

- Invest in a variety of reusable containers. You will need a few different sizes: medium or large ones can hold greens and veggies, and small ones can contain toppings. Small airtight containers with screw-on lids are excellent for holding dressings and watery veggies that can spill in transit. Canning jars make great shakers for blending dressings.

PREP

- Wash, prep and store greens as soon as you get home (turn to page 24 for a handy how-to). If they're ready to go in the fridge, you'll be able to assemble your salad efficiently even if you're bleary-eyed in the morning.

- Wash and cut up veggies after the greens are prepped. Sturdy carrots, zucchini, broccoli and so on are great choices if you prep them ahead, and it saves time when you're rushing around before heading out the door.

- Stir up a tasty salad dressing that can last all week. Just ensure that it has an acidic component, such as lemon juice or vinegar, if it contains garlic. Dangerous bacteria can grow on garlic in an airless, oil-only environment.

PACK

- Keep wet and dry ingredients separate. Pack greens and dry veggies in one container, and juicy veggies in another to prevent your salad from getting soggy. Dressings and dry toppings, such as croutons, should also go in separate containers so the crunchy items stay crunchy.

- Add a cold pack or frozen juice box to your lunch bag if you're travelling a long distance. It will keep cold items within the food-safe temperature range.

ENJOY

- Toss everything together right before sitting down to lunch. Don't let the dressing sit too long on the greens before enjoying them—there's nothing nice about a wilted salad.

- Make mixing up your salad fun. Toss everything in a large airtight container and snap the lid on. Then shake until all the ingredients are mixed and coated with dressing. It's a terrific stress-buster in the middle of the day!

CUCUMBER COUSCOUS SALAD

THIS CRUNCHY SALAD IS THE VERY DEFINITION OF FRESH AND LIGHT. IT'S A TERRIFIC SIDE DISH TO ENJOY YEAR ROUND: IN THE SUMMER, CHOOSE NOT-TOO-LARGE FIELD CUCUMBERS AND PEEL OFF THE TOUGH SKIN; IN THE COOLER MONTHS, USE HOTHOUSE ENGLISH CUCUMBERS, WHICH DON'T REQUIRE PEELING.

METHOD

In large bowl, cover couscous with boiling water; let stand for 5 minutes. Fluff with fork; let cool. Add cucumber, radishes and green onions.

Thyme Cumin Dressing: Whisk together oil, lemon juice, thyme, garlic, cumin, salt and pepper. (*Make-ahead: Cover and refrigerate salad and dressing separately for up to 24 hours.*)

Toss dressing with salad. Divide lettuce leaves among six plates; spoon salad into lettuce cups. Sprinkle with toasted pine nuts.

INGREDIENTS

1 cup	whole wheat couscous
1 cup	boiling water
2 cups	diced English cucumber
½ cup	sliced radishes
2	green onions, sliced
6	leaves Boston lettuce
¼ cup	pine nuts or slivered almonds, toasted (see how-to, below, and tip, page 44)

Thyme Cumin Dressing:

3 tbsp	vegetable oil
2 tbsp	lemon juice
1 tbsp	chopped fresh thyme
1	clove garlic, minced
½ tsp	each ground cumin and salt
¼ tsp	pepper

HOW TO

TOAST PINE NUTS

In small dry skillet over medium-high heat, toast pine nuts, shaking pan constantly, until golden, about 3 minutes.

Makes 6 servings.

PER SERVING: about 228 cal, 7 g pro, 11 g total fat (1 g sat. fat), 29 g carb, 6 g fibre, 0 mg chol, 198 mg sodium. % RDI: 3% calcium, 15% iron, 2% vit A, 13% vit C, 10% folate.

BEAN, MUSHROOM AND WILTED SPINACH SALAD

WARM SALADS ARE A COSY, COMFORTING ALTERNATIVE TO FRESH ONES. THIS MIX OF CHICKPEAS, BEANS, SPINACH AND MUSHROOMS IS HEARTY ENOUGH TO MAKE A MEAL ON ITS OWN, BUT IT'S A LOVELY ADDITION TO A BUFFET AS WELL.

INGREDIENTS

225 g	yellow or green beans
1	pkg (170 g) baby spinach
3 tbsp	extra-virgin olive oil
1	small sweet onion, thinly sliced
225 g	cremini mushrooms
1	clove garlic, minced
¼ tsp	each salt and pepper
¼ tsp	dried thyme
1 cup	rinsed drained canned chickpeas
3 tbsp	white wine vinegar
4	hard-cooked eggs (see how-to, page 79), quartered
3 tbsp	shaved Asiago cheese

METHOD

In saucepan of boiling water, cook yellow beans until tender-crisp, about 2 minutes. Drain; set aside.

Meanwhile, place spinach in large bowl; set aside.

In large skillet, heat oil over medium-high heat; sauté onion until tender, about 5 minutes. Add mushrooms, garlic, salt, pepper and thyme; cook, stirring occasionally, until mushrooms are tender and golden, about 7 minutes.

Add yellow beans, chickpeas and vinegar; cook until heated through. Add to spinach, tossing to wilt and coat. Arrange salad on plates. Top with eggs; sprinkle with cheese.

Makes 4 servings.

PER SERVING: about 352 cal, 18 g pro, 18 g total fat (4 g sat. fat), 32 g carb, 10 g fibre, 190 mg chol, 530 mg sodium, 814 mg potassium. % RDI: 18% calcium, 31% iron, 51% vit A, 15% vit C, 76% folate.

LENTIL FETA SALAD

FETA CHEESE GIVES THIS MEDITERRANEAN SIDE DISH A RICH, SALTY TANG THAT COMPLEMENTS THE EARTHINESS OF THE LENTILS. THE SALAD KEEPS FOR UP TO TWO DAYS IN THE FRIDGE (SOME WOULD SAY IT GETS EVEN TASTIER AS IT STANDS), SO IT'S WORTH MAKING EXTRA TO ENJOY FOR LUNCH THE NEXT DAY.

136

INGREDIENTS

½ cup	slivered almonds
1 cup	dried green lentils
2	cloves garlic
¼ cup	extra-virgin olive oil
3 tbsp	red wine vinegar
1 tbsp	finely chopped fresh oregano
¼ tsp	each salt and pepper
1½ cups	diced English cucumber
1 cup	halved cherry tomatoes
½ cup	diced sweet or red onion
2 tbsp	chopped fresh parsley
¾ cup	crumbled feta cheese

METHOD

In small dry skillet, toast almonds over medium heat, stirring often, until golden, about 5 minutes. Set aside.

Bring large pot of salted water to boil. Add lentils and garlic; reduce heat and simmer until tender, about 20 minutes. Drain and rinse under cold water; drain again. Discard garlic.

In large bowl, whisk together oil, vinegar, oregano, salt and pepper. Add lentils, cucumber, tomatoes, onion and parsley; toss to coat. *(Make-ahead: Cover and refrigerate for up to 2 days.)*

Stir in almonds and all but ¼ cup of the feta cheese; garnish with remaining cheese.

TEST KITCHEN TIP

Oregano is an easy-to-grow kitchen herb that thrives even in small pots. It doesn't require much care, and you can even bring it inside over the winter and enjoy the fresh herb year-round. The leaves also dry very well—tie a bundle of sprigs and hang it upside down in a dry spot for a week or two. Then pull off the leaves and crumble them into pasta sauces and Mediterranean dishes.

Makes 6 servings.
PER SERVING: about 305 cal, 14 g pro, 18 g total fat (5 g sat. fat), 25 g carb, 6 g fibre, 17 mg chol, 532 mg sodium. % RDI: 14% calcium, 29% iron, 6% vit A, 13% vit C, 89% folate.

WARM CANNELLINI BEAN AND DANDELION SALAD

WHILE ALL PARTS OF THE DANDELION PLANT ARE EDIBLE, THE LEAVES ARE ALWAYS THE BEST. TO PREPARE THE GREENS, TRIM OFF THE ROOT ENDS, RINSE THE LEAVES WELL UNDER COLD RUNNING WATER AND SPIN DRY.

METHOD

Cut dandelion greens in half crosswise; set aside. In Dutch oven, heat oil over medium heat; cook onion and garlic, stirring occasionally, until golden, about 5 minutes.

Add prosciutto, oregano and hot pepper flakes; cook, stirring occasionally, until prosciutto is crisp, about 4 minutes.

Add dandelion greens; cook, stirring, for 2 minutes. Stir in wine and beans; cover and cook until greens are softened, about 5 minutes. Discard oregano. Let cool for 3 minutes.

In large bowl, toss together baby spinach, balsamic vinegar and dandelion mixture. Serve warm.

CHANGE IT UP
WARM FAVA BEAN AND DANDELION SALAD

Substitute fava beans for the cannellini beans.

INGREDIENTS

1	bunch (about 280 g) dandelion greens, trimmed
¼ cup	extra-virgin olive oil
1	onion, chopped
6	cloves garlic, smashed
3	slices prosciutto, thinly sliced crosswise
5	sprigs fresh oregano
¼ tsp	hot pepper flakes
⅓ cup	white wine
1	can (540 mL) cannellini or white kidney beans, drained and rinsed
8 cups	lightly packed baby spinach
4 tsp	balsamic vinegar

PHOTO
PAGE 138

Makes 8 servings.

PER SERVING: about 159 cal, 7 g pro, 8 g total fat (1 g sat. fat), 15 g carb, 6 g fibre, 6 mg chol, 332 mg sodium, 499 mg potassium. % RDI: 11% calcium, 19% iron, 73% vit A, 35% vit C, 39% folate.

WARM CANNELLINI BEAN
AND DANDELION SALAD

PAGE 137

BROWN RICE AND GRILLED VEGETABLE SALAD

A HERBACEOUS BRIGHT GREEN SAUCE IS THE STAR OF THIS VEGGIE-DENSE GRAIN SALAD.
YOU'LL WANT TO EAT THAT SAUCE ON EVERYTHING! LOOK FOR WHOLE GRAIN BROWN RICE THAT'S READY IN 20 MINUTES;
IT'S A CONVENIENT WAY TO INCORPORATE WHOLE GRAINS INTO EVERYDAY DINNERS.

INGREDIENTS

1 cup	whole grain 20-minute brown rice (such as Uncle Ben's)
2	zucchini, cut lengthwise in ½-inch (1 cm) thick slices
1	eggplant, cut lengthwise in ½-inch (1 cm) thick slices
1	sweet yellow or red pepper, halved
1	white onion, cut in ½-inch (1 cm) thick slices
⅓ cup	crumbled feta cheese (optional)

Green Sauce:

½ cup	fresh parsley leaves
½ cup	fresh cilantro leaves
¼ cup	fresh mint leaves
3 tbsp	extra-virgin olive oil
1 tbsp	rinsed drained capers
1 tbsp	lemon juice
2 tsp	Dijon mustard
½ tsp	each salt and pepper

METHOD

Green Sauce: In bowl and using immersion blender, purée together parsley, cilantro, mint, oil, capers, lemon juice, mustard, salt and pepper until smooth; set aside.

In large saucepan of boiling water, cook rice according to package directions. Drain; transfer to large bowl. Meanwhile, place zucchini, eggplant, yellow pepper and onion on greased grill over medium-high heat; close lid and grill, turning once, until tender, 12 to 15 minutes. Let cool enough to handle.

Coarsely chop vegetables; toss with rice. Sprinkle with feta cheese (if using). Serve with green sauce.

Makes 4 servings.
PER SERVING: about 368 cal, 7 g pro, 12 g total fat (2 g sat. fat), 61 g carb, 7 g fibre, 0 mg chol, 422 mg sodium, 786 mg potassium. % RDI: 7% calcium, 21% iron, 20% vit A, 108% vit C, 34% folate.

QUINOA TABBOULEH

MIDDLE EASTERN TABBOULEH IS USUALLY MADE WITH BULGUR (A PARBOILED FORM OF WHEAT), WHICH CONTAINS GLUTEN. BY USING QUINOA, A SEED THAT IS ALSO AN EXCELLENT SOURCE OF IRON, THIS SALAD BECOMES A REFRESHING OPTION FOR PEOPLE WHO CAN'T CONSUME GLUTEN.

METHOD

In saucepan, bring 1½ cups water to boil; add quinoa and return to boil. Reduce heat, cover and simmer until no liquid remains, about 18 minutes. Remove from heat; fluff with fork. Transfer to bowl; let cool.

Add parsley, cucumber, green onions, mint and tomato.

Dressing: Whisk together lemon juice, oil, salt and pepper; pour over quinoa mixture. Toss to coat. Serve at room temperature or cover and refrigerate for up to 1 hour.

INGREDIENTS

¾ cup	quinoa, rinsed and drained (see how-to, below)
1 cup	chopped fresh flat-leaf parsley
1 cup	chopped English cucumber
½ cup	chopped green onions
¼ cup	chopped fresh mint
1	tomato, seeded and chopped

Dressing:

3 tbsp	lemon juice
2 tbsp	extra-virgin olive oil
¼ tsp	each salt and pepper

HOW TO

PREPARE QUINOA FOR USE IN RECIPES

Quinoa is naturally coated with a bitter compound called saponin, which protects the seeds. Most commercial quinoa is labelled as ready to use right out of the box, but The Test Kitchen recommends rinsing it thoroughly under cold running water just to be sure any traces of bitterness are gone. Drain the quinoa well before proceeding with the recipe.

Makes 6 servings.

PER SERVING: about 135 cal, 4 g pro, 6 g total fat (1 g sat. fat), 18 g carb, 3 g fibre, 0 mg chol, 112 mg sodium, 335 mg potassium. % RDI: 4% calcium, 24% iron, 13% vit A, 33% vit C, 18% folate.

SUPER SUMMER WHOLE GRAIN SALAD

THIS SUPER-DELICIOUS, SUPER-NUTRITIOUS SALAD WILL BECOME YOUR GO-TO RECIPE THROUGHOUT THE SUMMER FOR BACKYARD BARBECUES, FAMILY GATHERINGS OR PICNICS AT THE BEACH. LOOK FOR PRECOOKED GRAIN AND LEGUME BLENDS IN THE GROCERY STORE NEAR THE RICE.

METHOD

In saucepan, bring 4 cups water to boil; stir in grain blend. Cook over medium-high heat until tender, 10 to 12 minutes. Drain and transfer to large bowl; let cool.

Add carrot, yellow pepper, zucchini, radishes, arugula and peas to grain blend.

Chive Citrus Vinaigrette: Meanwhile, in small bowl, whisk together orange juice, oil, vinegar, salt and pepper; stir in chives. Toss with salad; sprinkle with pepitas.

CHANGE IT UP

SUPER SUMMER GLUTEN-FREE WHOLE GRAIN SALAD

Replace five-grain blend with ¾ cup quinoa or brown rice, cooking according to package directions.

INGREDIENTS

1 cup	precooked five-grain blend (such as President's Choice)
1	carrot, diced
1	sweet yellow pepper, diced
1	small zucchini, diced
3	radishes, halved and thinly sliced
4 cups	lightly packed baby arugula
¾ cup	cooled cooked peas
⅓ cup	pepitas (see tip, page 218), toasted

Chive Citrus Vinaigrette:

3 tbsp	orange juice
2 tbsp	olive oil
1 tbsp	white wine vinegar
¼ tsp	each salt and pepper
¼ cup	chopped fresh chives

Makes 4 servings.
PER SERVING: about 324 cal, 11 g pro, 13 g total fat (2 g sat. fat), 23 g carb, 6 g fibre, 0 mg chol, 187 mg sodium, 440 mg potassium. % RDI: 6% calcium, 26% iron, 37% vit A, 122% vit C, 31% folate.

QUINOA AND CELERIAC SALAD

CELERIAC IS AN UNDERAPPRECIATED FALL VEGETABLE, MOSTLY DUE TO ITS STRANGE, KNOBBY EXTERIOR. DON'T BE SCARED BY ITS SIZE—TRIMMING REDUCES IT TO ABOUT TWO-THIRDS OF ITS ORIGINAL BULK. CELERIAC TURNS BROWN QUICKLY, SO BE SURE TO COAT IT WITH THE DRESSING RIGHT AFTER CUTTING IT.

INGREDIENTS

1 cup	quinoa, rinsed and drained (see how-to, page 141)
½ tsp	each salt and pepper
2 cups	grape tomatoes, halved
1 tbsp	olive oil
2 tsp	balsamic vinegar
⅓ cup	sunflower seeds
1	celeriac (about 565 g)
¼ cup	lemon juice
¼ cup	light mayonnaise
1 tbsp	Dijon mustard
Quarter	red onion, thinly sliced
¼ cup	chopped fresh dill

METHOD

In saucepan, bring 2 cups water to boil; add quinoa and ¼ tsp each of the salt and pepper. Reduce heat to medium-low; cover and simmer until tender and no liquid remains, about 12 minutes. Remove from heat; let stand for 15 minutes. Fluff with fork; let cool to room temperature.

Meanwhile, toss together tomatoes, 2 tsp of the oil, vinegar and a pinch each of the remaining salt and pepper. Roast, cut side up, on parchment paper–lined rimmed baking sheet in 375°F (190°C) oven until lightly browned and shrivelled, about 25 minutes. Let cool to room temperature.

Meanwhile, on separate rimmed baking sheet, spread sunflower seeds; add to oven and toast just until golden and fragrant, about 5 minutes. Let cool to room temperature.

Meanwhile, trim and peel celeriac. Using mandoline or sharp knife, julienne (see how-to, page 36). Place in large bowl; add lemon juice and remaining oil, salt and pepper. Toss well to coat. Stir in mayonnaise and mustard until blended.

Add cooled quinoa, red onion, half of the sunflower seeds and the dill; mix well. Garnish with remaining sunflower seeds and roasted tomatoes.

Makes 6 servings.

PER SERVING: about 249 cal, 7 g pro, 12 g total fat (2 g sat. fat), 32 g carb, 5 g fibre, 3 mg chol, 371 mg sodium, 617 mg potassium. % RDI: 6% calcium, 29% iron, 5% vit A, 25% vit C, 21% folate.

SUMMERTIME BARLEY SALAD

THIS YUMMY SWEET-AND-SAVOURY SALAD MAY APPEAR TO HAVE A LOT OF DRESSING, BUT THE BARLEY AND APRICOTS WILL ABSORB MOST OF IT WHILE IT STANDS, ADDING LOTS OF FLAVOUR.

INGREDIENTS

1¾ cups	pearl barley, rinsed and drained
1	clove garlic, minced
¼ cup	cider vinegar
2 tbsp	lemon juice
4 tsp	Dijon mustard
¾ tsp	salt
¼ tsp	pepper
¼ cup	extra-virgin olive oil
1 cup	diced medium or aged Gouda cheese
½ cup	diced dried apricots
⅓ cup	salted roasted pepitas (see tip, page 218)

METHOD

In large pot of boiling lightly salted water, cook barley according to package directions. Drain and rinse under cold water; drain well.

In large bowl, stir together garlic, vinegar, lemon juice, mustard, salt and pepper; slowly whisk in oil until emulsified. Add barley, Gouda cheese and apricots; toss to coat. Cover and refrigerate for 4 hours. (*Make-ahead: Refrigerate for up to 24 hours.*)

To serve, toss salad with pepitas.

TEST KITCHEN TIP

To give the finished salad an even fresher, greener edge, stir in ¼ cup chopped fresh parsley just before serving.

Makes 6 to 8 servings.

PER EACH OF 8 SERVINGS: about 351 cal, 10 g pro, 17 g total fat (5 g sat. fat), 43 g carb, 4 g fibre, 19 mg chol, 887 mg sodium, 322 mg potassium. % RDI: 13% calcium, 21% iron, 6% vit A, 2% vit C, 14% folate.

CLOCKWISE FROM TOP LEFT:
Fully Loaded Potato Salad (page 199),
Fennel and Parmesan Coleslaw (page 210),
Mediterranean Orzo Salad (page 166) and
Summertime Barley Salad (opposite).

Best Berry Vinegars and Vinaigrettes

STRAWBERRY BALSAMIC VINEGAR

Strawberries give this berry vinegar a surprising sweetness. Look for ripe local berries in early summer.

1½ cups white balsamic vinegar
1 cup halved hulled fresh strawberries
1 tsp black peppercorns
5 fresh basil leaves
Pinch salt

In saucepan, combine vinegar with strawberries, mashing slightly. Add peppercorns, basil and salt; bring to boil. Reduce heat and simmer for 2 minutes. Remove from heat; let cool completely. Discard basil leaves.

Seal in heatproof jar. Refrigerate for 1 week. Strain through cheesecloth-lined sieve into sterilized jar. Seal and refrigerate for up to 1 month.

Makes about 1⅓ cups.

PER 1 TBSP: about 18 cal, trace pro, 0 g total fat (0 g sat. fat), 4 g carb, 0 g fibre, 0 mg chol, 4 mg sodium, 32 mg potassium. % RDI: 1% calcium, 1% iron, 5% vit C.

RASPBERRY BALSAMIC VINEGAR

Scraping off the white pith from the orange zest keeps the vinegar from developing a bitter edge.

1½ cups white balsamic vinegar
1 cup fresh raspberries
1 strip orange zest
5 large fresh mint leaves
Pinch salt

In saucepan, combine vinegar with raspberries, mashing slightly. Scrape any pith off orange zest; add to pan along with mint and salt. Bring to boil; reduce heat and simmer for 2 minutes. Remove from heat; let cool completely. Discard orange zest and mint.

Seal in heatproof jar. Refrigerate for 1 week. Strain through cheesecloth-lined sieve into sterilized jar. Seal and refrigerate for up to 1 month.

Makes about 1⅓ cups.

PER 1 TBSP: about 17 cal, trace pro, 0 g total fat (0 g sat. fat), 3 g carb, 0 g fibre, 0 mg chol, 4 mg sodium, 27 mg potassium. % RDI: 1% calcium, 1% iron, 2% vit C.

CHANGE IT UP
BLUEBERRY BALSAMIC VINEGAR

Substitute blueberries for raspberries, lemon zest for orange zest and 2 sprigs fresh thyme for mint.

BASIC BERRY VINAIGRETTE

This is the go-to recipe for making berry vinaigrette. This dressing is lovely on mixed greens and spinach salads, especially ones with fruit in them.

2 tbsp extra-virgin olive oil
2 tbsp Strawberry, Raspberry or Blueberry Balsamic Vinegar (recipes, left)
1 tbsp vegetable oil
1 small shallot, minced
Pinch each salt and pepper
Pinch granulated sugar

In small glass measure, whisk together olive oil, vinegar, vegetable oil, shallot, salt, pepper and sugar. Store in airtight container for up to 24 hours.

Makes ⅓ cup.

PER 1 TBSP: about 75 cal, trace pro, 8 g total fat (1 g sat. fat), 2 g carb, 0 g fibre, 0 mg chol, 2 mg sodium, 17 mg potassium. % RDI: 1% iron, 2% vit C.

ROASTED PEPPER, WHITE BEAN AND GOAT CHEESE SALAD

ROASTED GARLIC BRINGS A LOVELY CREAMINESS AND SUBTLE SWEETNESS TO THIS SIMPLE SALAD'S LEMONY VINAIGRETTE. THE BEANS AND CHEESE GIVE IT A HEARTY FEEL, MAKING IT AN EASY, COMPLETE DINNER.

149

METHOD

Wrap garlic in foil; place on foil-lined rimmed baking sheet along with red peppers. Roast in 425°F (220°C) oven, turning peppers occasionally, until skins are blistered, about 25 minutes for garlic, 35 minutes for peppers.

Transfer peppers to bowl; cover with plastic wrap and let stand for 15 minutes. Peel, seed and chop peppers; transfer to clean bowl. Add beans.

Let garlic cool enough to handle; squeeze into small bowl. Whisk in oil, lemon juice, thyme, vinegar, mustard, salt and pepper until smooth. Pour over red pepper mixture; toss to coat. Sprinkle with goat cheese.

INGREDIENTS

4	cloves garlic (unpeeled)
3	sweet red peppers
1	can (540 mL) navy beans or white kidney beans, drained and rinsed
¼ cup	extra-virgin olive oil
4 tsp	lemon juice
2 tsp	chopped fresh thyme
2 tsp	white wine vinegar
½ tsp	Dijon mustard
½ tsp	salt
¼ tsp	pepper
½ cup	crumbled soft goat cheese

TEST KITCHEN TIP

Red peppers add a punch of colour and sweetness to this otherwise cream-coloured salad. Orange or yellow peppers are just as sweet; substitute them for the red or use a mix of all three if you prefer.

Makes 4 servings.

PER SERVING: about 329 cal, 13 g pro, 18 g total fat (5 g sat. fat), 31 g carb, 3 g fibre, 9 mg chol, 777 mg sodium, 434 mg potassium. % RDI: 8% calcium, 19% iron, 38% vit A, 250% vit C, 34% folate.

MEDITERRANEAN BARLEY RICE SALAD

THIS IS A GORGEOUS SALAD TO BRING TO A POTLUCK OR PARTY. THE COMBINATION OF COLOURS, TEXTURES, AROMAS AND FLAVOURS MAKES IT A TREAT FOR THE SENSES. RINSING THE BARLEY AND THE RICE ENSURES THE GRAINS WILL BE FLUFFY (NOT STICKY) WHEN COOKED.

150

INGREDIENTS

1 cup	pearl barley, rinsed and drained
1 cup	basmati rice, rinsed and drained
3 cups	cherry tomatoes
Half	large red onion
1	sweet red pepper
1	English cucumber
4 cups	baby spinach, coarsely chopped
1	pkg (200 g) feta cheese, crumbled

Dressing:

½ cup	extra-virgin olive oil
½ cup	lemon juice
1 tsp	dried oregano
1 tsp	salt
½ tsp	pepper

METHOD

In saucepan of boiling salted water, cook barley until tender, about 20 minutes. Drain and rinse under cold water; drain well. Let stand for 10 minutes to dry. Transfer to large bowl.

Meanwhile, in separate saucepan, bring 1½ cups salted water to boil. Add rice; cover, reduce heat and simmer until tender and no liquid remains, about 15 minutes. Let stand for 5 minutes. Add to barley mixture; let cool.

Cut tomatoes in half; add to barley mixture. Cut onion, red pepper and cucumber into 1-inch (2.5 cm) chunks; add to barley mixture. Toss to combine.

Dressing: Whisk together oil, lemon juice, oregano, salt and pepper; pour over salad. Toss to coat. Refrigerate for 30 minutes. *(Make-ahead: Refrigerate for up to 24 hours.)*

Just before serving, stir in spinach and feta cheese.

Makes 12 to 16 servings.
PER EACH OF 16 SERVINGS: about 197 cal, 4 g pro, 10 g total fat (3 g sat. fat), 24 g carb, 2 g fibre, 12 mg chol, 554 mg sodium, 234 mg potassium. % RDI: 8% calcium, 8% iron, 14% vit A, 38% vit C, 16% folate.

BLACK BEAN AND CORN SALAD
with monterey jack cheese

BLACK BEANS ARE A GREAT SOURCE OF FIBRE AND ARE AT THEIR BEST WHEN COMBINED WITH SOUTHWESTERN INGREDIENTS IN A SALAD. TO KICK UP THE HEAT A NOTCH, ADD A DICED SEEDED JALAPEÑO PEPPER.

INGREDIENTS

2 tbsp	lime juice
2 tbsp	olive oil
1 tbsp	liquid honey
1	clove garlic, minced
1 tsp	chili powder
1	can (540 mL) black beans, drained and rinsed
1 cup	frozen corn kernels, cooked and cooled
½ cup	diced red onion
½ cup	cubed Monterey Jack cheese
2 tbsp	chopped fresh cilantro

METHOD

In bowl, whisk together lime juice, oil, honey, garlic and chili powder until blended.

Add black beans, corn, onion, Monterey Jack cheese and cilantro; toss to coat.

TEST KITCHEN TIP

Home-cooked beans have a drier, firmer texture than canned beans, which can be nice in salads like this. For this dish, you'll need 2 cups cooked black beans. Just follow the prep and cooking instructions in Cooking Dried Beans, page 116.

Makes 4 servings.

PER SERVING: about 282 cal, 12 g pro, 13 g total fat (4 g sat. fat), 33 g carb, 9 g fibre, 15 mg chol, 454 mg sodium, 438 mg potassium. % RDI: 15% calcium, 16% iron, 7% vit A, 15% vit C, 36% folate.

WILD RICE AND LENTIL SALAD

WILD RICE IS AS CANADIAN AS MAPLE SYRUP, PLUS IT'S HIGH IN FIBRE AND PROTEIN (WITH DOUBLE THAT OF BROWN RICE). IT'S ALSO GLUTEN-FREE! BLENDING THE RICE WITH TRADITIONAL INDIAN SPICES, SWEET CURRANTS AND CRUNCHY ALMONDS MAKES A SALAD FIT FOR ANY TIME OF YEAR AND ANY SORT OF OCCASION.

METHOD

In small saucepan, bring 4 cups water and wild rice to boil; reduce heat, cover and simmer until most of the rice is split and tender, about 45 minutes. Remove from heat; let stand, covered, for 5 minutes. Drain.

Meanwhile, in large bowl, whisk together coriander, cumin, turmeric, sugar, cinnamon, salt and pepper. Whisk in vinegar and olive oil.

Stir in lentils, red onion, parsley, currants and wild rice. (Make-ahead: Refrigerate in airtight container for up to 2 days.) Stir in sliced almonds.

INGREDIENTS

1 cup	wild rice, rinsed and drained
1 tsp	ground coriander
1 tsp	ground cumin
½ tsp	ground turmeric
½ tsp	granulated sugar
¼ tsp	cinnamon
¼ tsp	each salt and pepper
¼ cup	vinegar
¼ cup	olive oil
1	can (540 mL) lentils, drained and rinsed
1 cup	diced red onion
½ cup	chopped fresh parsley
¼ cup	dried currants
½ cup	sliced almonds, toasted (see tip, page 44)

Makes 8 to 10 servings.

PER EACH OF 10 SERVINGS: about 199 cal, 7 g pro, 8 g total fat (1 g sat. fat), 26 g carb, 4 g fibre, 0 mg chol, 159 mg sodium, 316 mg potassium. % RDI: 3% calcium, 18% iron, 3% vit A, 10% vit C, 44% folate.

WATERCRESS AND ORANGE COUSCOUS SALAD

PEPPERY WATERCRESS ISN'T JUST FOR TEA SANDWICHES. IT MAKES THE PERFECT SALAD GREEN IF YOU SNAP OFF THE MOST TENDER STALKS AND LEAVES; TOSS THEM WITH THE DRESSING JUST BEFORE SERVING TO KEEP THEM FROM WILTING. TURN THIS APPETIZER OR SIDE SALAD INTO A HEARTY MEAL BY TOPPING IT WITH A SALMON FILLET OR CHICKEN BREAST.

155

METHOD

Whisk together oil, vinegar, mustard, honey, salt and pepper. Set aside.

Working over bowl, cut off rind and outer membrane of oranges; cut between membrane and pulp to release sections into bowl. Squeeze juice from remaining membranes into bowl.

Strain juice from oranges into liquid measure; add enough water to make 1⅓ cups. Pour into small saucepan; bring to boil.

Place couscous in clean bowl; pour boiling orange juice mixture over top. Cover with plastic wrap and let stand until liquid is absorbed, about 5 minutes. Fluff with fork; toss with ¼ cup of the dressing. Spread in serving dish.

In large bowl, toss together watercress, red onion, orange segments and remaining dressing. Arrange over couscous. Gently break goat cheese into chunks; sprinkle over top.

INGREDIENTS

¼ cup	olive oil
3 tbsp	red wine vinegar
2 tsp	Dijon mustard
2 tsp	liquid honey
¼ tsp	each salt and pepper
2	navel oranges
1⅓ cups	whole wheat couscous
1	bunch watercress, trimmed
¼ cup	red onion, thinly sliced
¼ cup	soft goat cheese

Makes 4 servings.

PER SERVING: about 437 cal, 13 g pro, 18 g total fat (4 g sat. fat), 60 g carb, 9 g fibre, 7 mg chol, 245 mg sodium, 311 mg potassium. % RDI: 9% calcium, 19% iron, 14% vit A, 62% vit C, 13% folate.

DILL AND FETA QUINOA SALAD

MANY PEOPLE DON'T THINK TO ADD HERBS TO SALADS, BUT THEY GIVE THEM A FRESH, GREEN NOTE THAT'S ADDICTIVE. HERE, DILL ADDS A LUSH, GRASSY FLAVOUR THAT COMPLEMENTS THE CREAMY FETA CHEESE. THIS SALAD IS GREAT AS A SIDE DISH BUT IT ALSO MAKES A TASTY, LIGHT LUNCH.

156

INGREDIENTS

⅔ cup	quinoa, rinsed and drained (see how-to, page 141)
¼ cup	olive oil
2 tbsp	red wine vinegar
¼ tsp	each salt and pepper
2	carrots, shredded
2	zucchini, shredded
½ cup	chopped fresh dill
½ cup	crumbled feta cheese

METHOD

In saucepan, bring 1⅓ cups water and quinoa to boil; reduce heat, cover and simmer for 12 minutes. Fluff with fork; let cool.

In large bowl, whisk together oil, vinegar, salt and pepper.

Add cooled quinoa, carrots, zucchini, dill and feta cheese; toss until well combined.

TEST KITCHEN TIP

Dill is another easy-to-grow kitchen herb. It does well in poor soil and can tolerate quite a bit of neglect, though it does like a thorough watering in hot weather. It's a lovely herb to grow in pots on a deck or balcony, too. The feathery leaves are a perfect match for salads (especially ones made with cucumbers), fish dishes and eggs. The seeds can be dried and added to potato salads and pickles (along with the yellow flowers, called dill heads). Fresh dill keeps its bright flavour better when it's not cooked; adding it fresh to salads like this one is ideal.

Makes 4 servings.

PER SERVING: about 281 cal, 7 g pro, 19 g total fat (5 g sat. fat), 22 g carb, 4 g fibre, 17 mg chol, 250 mg sodium, 510 mg potassium. % RDI: 12% calcium, 13% iron, 65% vit A, 33% vit C, 32% folate.

Growing Herbs for Salads

Fresh herbs give salads dimension by adding a vibrant hit of flavour. And most tolerate a lot of benign neglect in the garden. Here's how to grow an aromatic kitchen garden packed with these tasty ingredients.

TYPES OF HERBS

Growing herbs is a practical pleasure. The plants are culinarily useful, and each has a certain beauty, aroma and flavour that enhance salads and dressings. Many people begin their gardening love affair with a small patch or pot of these easy-to-grow plants. There are three categories of herbs: annuals, biennials and perennials.

- **Annuals:** Soft-stemmed herbs (such as basil, chervil and cilantro) need to be reseeded or replanted every spring. Sow seeds of hardy annuals, such as chervil, as soon as the ground can be worked in early spring. For more tender annuals, such as basil, wait until all danger of frost has cleared.

- **Biennials:** Biennials, such as parsley, can be hardier than annuals and may survive into a second season (if the winter isn't too harsh), then die.

- **Perennials:** Woody-stemmed plants (such as rosemary, thyme, sage and bay) are perennials, coming up each year in the same spot. Protect them over the winter by enclosing them in a plastic-covered A-frame. Start seeds about one month before the last frost date.

Regardless of type, herbs aren't fussy about their growing environment; some (such as oregano) prefer near-drought conditions similar to their Mediterranean origins. To be safe, though, and for guaranteed success, plant herbs in a sunny location in fertile, well-drained soil. For container gardening, keep soil moist, because pots dry out fast.

HOW HERBS HELP OTHER PLANTS

With plants—as with people—good company seems to make life better. Paired with the appropriate plants, herbs can keep your garden almost carefree. Many repel pests, even as they attract birds and other beneficial visitors.

- **Basil** planted beside tomatoes improves their growth and flavour, and repels tomato hornworms and thrips.

- **Chives** improve the taste of carrots and tomatoes, help deter aphids on sunflowers and tomatoes, reduce black spots on roses, and control apple scab.

- **Lavender** attracts pollinators, such as bees and butterflies, and helps deter mice, moths, rabbits, mosquitoes and ticks.

- **Mint** (watch its invasive tendencies!) is a great companion for cabbage and tomatoes since it helps repel ants, cabbage moths, flea beetles and rodents.

- **Oregano,** a friend to broccoli, cabbage and cauliflower, protects against cabbage butterflies and scares away cucumber beetles.

- **Thyme** is a longtime enemy of cabbage worms.

WARM LENTIL AND CARROT SALAD

WARM LENTILS SOAK UP A SIMPLE OIL-AND-VINEGAR DRESSING REALLY WELL.
IF YOU DON'T HAVE BALSAMIC VINEGAR IN YOUR PANTRY, SUBSTITUTE RED WINE VINEGAR;
THE SALAD WILL BE JUST A TINY BIT ON THE TART SIDE BUT JUST AS TASTY.

158

INGREDIENTS

1 cup	dried green lentils
¼ cup	extra-virgin olive oil
¼ cup	balsamic vinegar
2	small cloves garlic, minced
¼ tsp	each salt and pepper
2	carrots, diced
2	green onions, chopped

METHOD

In large saucepan of boiling water, cook lentils until tender, about 25 minutes. Drain.

Meanwhile, in bowl, whisk together oil, vinegar, garlic, salt and pepper; add lentils, carrots and green onions. Toss to coat.

In The Test Kitchen, we assume carrots are peeled before they're added to recipes. But some people prefer to skip this step, and it's actually not a bad idea. Most fruits and vegetables contain extra nutrients in their peels, and carrots are no exception. They can be gritty, though, especially when they're freshly picked from a backyard garden. If you want to omit peeling carrots, just make sure they're well scrubbed. Use a stiff vegetable brush, and get all the grit out of the tiny cracks on the surface. Nothing is more of a bummer than getting a bite of dirt in a beautifully made salad!

Makes 2 servings.
PER SERVING: about 314 cal, 13 g pro, 14 g total fat (2 g sat. fat), 35 g carb, 7 g fibre, 0 mg chol, 33 mg sodium, 673 mg potassium. % RDI: 5% calcium, 36% iron, 61% vit A, 10% vit C, 120% folate.

EDAMAME, RED PEPPER AND CORN SALAD

THIS RAINBOW-HUED DISH IS A MUST-EAT IN THE SUMMER, BECAUSE YOU CAN ENJOY USING FRESH LOCAL SWEET PEPPERS AND SWEET CORN WHEN THEY'RE AT THEIR PEAK RIPENESS. JUST BOIL UP A COUPLE OF EXTRA COBS OF CORN AND CUT OFF THE KERNELS THE NIGHT BEFORE YOU WANT TO MAKE THIS DISH.

159

METHOD

In large bowl, whisk together soy sauce, sesame oil, honey and garlic until well blended.

Add edamame, red pepper and corn kernels; toss to coat.

INGREDIENTS

2 tsp	sodium-reduced soy sauce
1 tsp	sesame oil
1 tsp	liquid honey
1	clove garlic, minced
1 cup	frozen shelled edamame, thawed and drained
1 cup	diced sweet red pepper
½ cup	fresh or frozen corn kernels, cooked and cooled

TEST KITCHEN TIP

Using shelled edamame (Japanese green soybeans) ups the convenience factor of this dish; look for bags of them in your grocer's freezer section. They shorten the prep time for this salad to just five minutes, which is excellent for a busy weeknight.

Makes 4 servings.

PER SERVING: about 78 cal, 4 g pro, 3 g total fat (trace sat. fat), 11 g carb, 2 g fibre, 0 mg chol, 92 mg sodium, 272 mg potassium. % RDI: 2% calcium, 6% iron, 12% vit A, 125% vit C, 47% folate.

GRILLED CHICKEN BARLEY SALAD

SEEMS LIKE EVERYONE LOVES GRILLED CHICKEN ON A SALAD. HERE, THE SALAD ISN'T A GREEN ONE, BUT RATHER ONE MADE WITH TENDER PEARL BARLEY AND GRAPE TOMATOES. IT'S GREAT FOR LUNCH OR DINNER.

METHOD

Italian Herb Vinaigrette: In large bowl, whisk together oil, vinegar, mustard, Italian herb seasoning, salt and pepper. Transfer 2 tbsp to large shallow dish; add chicken, turning to coat. Cover and refrigerate for 10 minutes. (*Make-ahead: Refrigerate for up to 8 hours.*)

Meanwhile, in saucepan of boiling water, cover and cook barley for 15 minutes. Add green beans; cook until beans are tender-crisp and barley is tender, about 5 minutes. Drain; toss with remaining vinaigrette.

Place chicken on greased grill over medium-high heat; close lid and grill, turning once, until no longer pink inside, about 10 minutes. Cut into cubes.

Add chicken to barley mixture. Add tomatoes, onion and basil; toss to coat.

INGREDIENTS

2	boneless skinless chicken breasts
⅔ cup	pearl barley
1½ cups	chopped green beans
1 cup	grape tomatoes, halved
¼ cup	minced red onion
2 tbsp	chopped fresh basil

Italian Herb Vinaigrette:

¼ cup	extra-virgin olive oil
2 tbsp	wine vinegar
1 tbsp	Dijon mustard
½ tsp	dried Italian herb seasoning
¼ tsp	each salt and pepper

Makes 4 servings.

PER SERVING: about 340 cal, 19 g pro, 15 g total fat (2 g sat. fat), 33 g carb, 4 g fibre, 39 mg chol, 236 mg sodium. % RDI: 4% calcium, 16% iron, 7% vit A, 13% vit C, 16% folate.

BEEF, BARLEY AND CORN SALAD

GRILLED BEEF PAIRED WITH CRISP SALAD IS A SUMMERTIME MATCH MADE IN HEAVEN.
STRIP LOIN STEAK IS A GOOD CHOICE FOR THIS DISH: IT'S TENDER AND DOESN'T
REQUIRE A LONG TIME IN THE MARINADE TO YIELD JUICY RESULTS.

INGREDIENTS

2 tbsp	vegetable oil
1 tsp	chili powder
½ tsp	each salt and pepper
2	cloves garlic, minced
450 g	beef strip loin grilling steak, 1 inch (2.5 cm) thick
4 cups	shredded red leaf lettuce

Barley and Corn Salad:

½ cup	pearl barley
1½ cups	fresh or frozen corn kernels, cooked and cooled
1½ cups	chopped tomatoes
⅓ cup	chopped fresh cilantro
⅓ cup	chopped red onion
3 tbsp	extra-virgin olive oil
3 tbsp	lime juice
¾ tsp	ground cumin
¼ tsp	salt

METHOD

Barley and Corn Salad: In saucepan of boiling water, cover and cook barley until tender, about 20 minutes. Let cool. In large bowl, combine cooled barley, corn, tomatoes, cilantro, red onion, oil, lime juice, cumin and salt; toss to coat.

Meanwhile, stir together oil, chili powder, salt, pepper and garlic; brush all over steak. Let stand for 15 minutes.

Place steak on greased grill over medium-high heat; close lid and grill, turning once, until medium-rare, about 8 minutes. Transfer to cutting board and tent with foil; let stand for 5 minutes before thinly slicing across the grain.

Divide lettuce among four plates; top with barley salad. Arrange steak over top.

Makes 4 servings.
PER SERVING: about 505 cal, 31 g pro, 24 g total fat (5 g sat. fat), 44 g carb, 6 g fibre, 56 mg chol, 509 mg sodium. % RDI: 4% calcium, 34% iron, 20% vit A, 27% vit C, 33% folate.

164

PASTA, POTATO, & SLAW

RECIPES

MEDITERRANEAN ORZO SALAD

THIS IS A GREAT EXAMPLE OF A DISH THAT CONTAINS SIMPLE MEDITERRANEAN INGREDIENTS.
IT'S ESPECIALLY TASTY MADE WITH GOOD-QUALITY OLIVE OIL, SO SPLURGE A LITTLE NEXT TIME YOU GO
SHOPPING. STIR THE FINISHED SALAD LIGHTLY WITH A FORK BEFORE SERVING TO LOOSEN THE PASTA.

166

INGREDIENTS

2 cups	orzo pasta
¼ cup	lemon juice
¼ cup	extra-virgin olive oil
1 tsp	liquid honey
½ tsp	each salt and pepper
Pinch	dried oregano
1	sweet red pepper, diced
1 cup	diced cored English cucumber
¾ cup	crumbled feta cheese
⅓ cup	chopped Kalamata olives
⅓ cup	chopped drained oil-packed sun-dried tomatoes
¼ cup	chopped fresh parsley
¼ cup	diced red onion

METHOD

In large pot of boiling lightly salted water, cook orzo according to package directions. Drain and rinse under cold water; drain well.

In large bowl, whisk together lemon juice, oil, honey, salt, pepper and oregano. Add orzo, red pepper, cucumber, feta cheese, olives, sun-dried tomatoes, parsley and red onion; stir to coat. *(Make-ahead: Cover and refrigerate for up to 24 hours.)*

TEST KITCHEN TIP

To pit several olives at once before chopping them, place olives on a cutting board and lightly crush with the bottom of a small saucepan to expose the pits, then pick them out.

PHOTO PAGE 147

Makes 6 to 8 servings.

PER EACH OF 8 SERVINGS: about 286 cal, 8 g pro, 12 g total fat (3 g sat. fat), 37 g carb, 3 g fibre, 13 mg chol, 514 mg sodium, 194 mg potassium. % RDI: 8% calcium, 8% iron, 9% vit A, 63% vit C, 10% folate.

ROASTED PEPPER AND CHEESE TORTELLINI SALAD

FRESH INGREDIENTS, READY-MADE PASTA AND A QUICK DRESSING COME TOGETHER SO EASILY AND SO DELICIOUSLY IN THIS HEARTY DISH. KEEP THIS RECIPE CLOSE AT HAND FOR BUSY WEEKNIGHT DINNERS OR PARTIES.

METHOD

On foil-lined rimmed baking sheet, broil red and green peppers, turning occasionally, until skins are blackened, about 15 minutes. Let cool enough to handle. Peel off blackened skins; core and seed. Cut into ¾-inch (2 cm) pieces.

Meanwhile, in large pot of boiling water, cook tortellini according to package directions; drain. Set aside.

In large bowl, whisk together vinegar, oil, garlic, thyme, mustard, salt, pepper and hot pepper flakes. Stir in roasted peppers, tortellini and pine nuts to coat. *(Make-ahead: Refrigerate in airtight container for up to 2 days.)*

INGREDIENTS

2	sweet red and/or yellow peppers
1	sweet green pepper
1	pkg (350 g) fresh cheese tortellini
3 tbsp	red wine vinegar
3 tbsp	extra-virgin olive oil
1	clove garlic, minced
½ tsp	dried thyme
½ tsp	Dijon mustard
Pinch	each salt and pepper
Pinch	hot pepper flakes
¼ cup	pine nuts, toasted (see how-to, page 133)

Makes 4 servings.

PER SERVING: about 508 cal, 13 g pro, 22 g total fat (5 g sat. fat), 61 g carb, 5 g fibre, 49 mg chol, 984 mg sodium. % RDI: 10% calcium, 19% iron, 22% vit A, 198% vit C, 8% folate.

TANGY MACARONI SALAD

MACARONI SALAD IS ONE OF THOSE POTLUCK STAPLES WITH TREMENDOUS
NOSTALGIC APPEAL. THIS VERSION GETS DRESSED UP WITH A LITTLE COLOURFUL PIMIENTO AND
A ZINGY SHALLOT VINAIGRETTE, MAKING IT FUN FOR CASUAL ENTERTAINING.

168

INGREDIENTS

4 cups	elbow macaroni
1 cup	diced celery
¼ cup	chopped drained pimientos

Shallot Dressing:

½ cup	finely chopped shallots or green onions
¼ cup	white wine vinegar
¾ tsp	salt
⅔ cup	mayonnaise
1 tbsp	granulated sugar
2 tsp	Dijon mustard
¼ tsp	pepper

METHOD

Shallot Dressing: In large bowl, combine shallots, vinegar and salt; let stand for 10 minutes. Stir in mayonnaise, sugar, mustard and pepper.

Meanwhile, in large pot of boiling salted water, cook pasta according to package directions until al dente. Drain and rinse under cold water; drain well. Add to dressing.

Add celery and pimientos; toss to coat evenly. Cover and refrigerate for 1 hour. *(Make-ahead: Refrigerate for up to 24 hours.)*

Makes 12 servings.

PER SERVING: about 230 cal, 5 g pro, 10 g total fat (2 g sat. fat), 29 g carb, 2 g fibre, 5 mg chol, 325 mg sodium, 90 mg potassium. % RDI: 2% calcium, 11% iron, 3% vit A, 10% vit C, 35% folate.

Making the Perfect Pasta Salad

Creating this picnic and barbecue staple is easy with the right ingredients and advice. Here's how.

THE BEST PASTA FOR THE SALAD

When it comes to variety, pasta shapes are nearly unlimited, from tiny dots to long ribbons to thick ringlets. Many come in different colours, too. And now there is pasta made in all those shapes from all sorts of different grains: wheat (whole and refined), spelt, kamut, white and brown rice, and many more. So which varieties should you choose for your pasta salads?

- **Small pastas** are versatile: They are lovely with simple vinaigrettes and pair well with chunky ingredients in salads. They look delicate and more elegant than larger types. Try orzo, ditalini, small shells and the newly popular Israeli couscous.

- **Short pastas** are great for salads, with both creamy dressings and vinaigrettes. They also work well with chunky chopped vegetables, meats, cheeses and beans. Ridged and swirly varieties are great at hanging on to small pieces of other ingredients, and dressings cling to their whirls and folds. Fun options are macaroni, fusilli, rotini, medium shells, penne and farfalle (bow ties).

- **Long pastas** go well with thinly sliced vegetables, meats, cheeses, shredded fresh herbs and oil-based vinaigrettes. Typical Italian pastas, such as spaghetti, linguine and fettuccine fall into this category, as do Asian noodles, such as curly chuka soba, buckwheat soba, somen, rice sticks and dried rice vermicelli.

- **Filled pastas** aren't as commonly used in pasta salads, but they are every bit as tasty. Fresh cheese-filled tortellini and ravioli, especially bite-size varieties, make pretty additions.

PASTA SALAD PREP FOR PARTIES

Pasta salads are great to make ahead and are absolutely the best for large groups. If you're making one in advance, rinse the hot cooked pasta under cold water to stop the cooking process. Then drain it well before adding it to the other ingredients. Make sure to shake out any excess cooking liquid, especially from tubular or swirly pastas, which can hang on to moisture and water down the dressing.

Pasta is absorbent and soaks up liquids as it stands. If you add dressing too far in advance, a pasta salad can get a little dry or sticky later. The make-aheads in our recipes ensure great-tasting results, especially for leftovers, but if you're making your salad ahead for a special event, adding the dressing just before serving ensures maximum moisture and flavour.

CHANGE IT UP

If you need a versatile dish that you can take to parties and potlucks, pasta salad is a no-brainer. Once you've found a few recipes you like, experiment with them, using the same proportions of similar ingredients. Swap in different pasta shapes, oils, vinegars, vegetables and seasonings. Or add a fresh hit of flavour with a handful of chopped fresh herbs. Let your imagination run wild.

GRILLED VEGETABLE PASTA SALAD

THE CARAMELIZED GOODNESS OF GRILLED VEGGIES IS IDEALLY MATCHED WITH A SIMPLE, TANGY VINAIGRETTE. ADD IN SOME CHEWY WHOLE WHEAT PASTA, AND YOU HAVE A FIBRE-PACKED SIDE DISH THAT DELIVERS A NUTRITIONAL WALLOP ALONG WITH GREAT TASTE.

METHOD

In large bowl, whisk together parsley, basil, oil, vinegar, garlic, salt and pepper; set aside.

Place mushrooms, red onion and zucchini on greased grill over medium-high heat; close lid and grill, turning once, until tender-crisp, 5 to 10 minutes. Cut mushrooms and onion into ½-inch (1 cm) chunks. Cut zucchini crosswise into ½-inch (1 cm) thick slices. Add vegetables to dressing; toss to coat.

Meanwhile, in large pot of boiling salted water, cook pasta according to package directions until al dente. Drain and rinse under cold water; drain well.

Add pasta, tomatoes, artichokes and olives to vegetable mixture; toss to combine. Sprinkle with Parmesan cheese.

INGREDIENTS

⅓ cup	chopped fresh parsley
⅓ cup	chopped fresh basil
⅓ cup	extra-virgin olive oil
¼ cup	red or white wine vinegar
1	clove garlic, minced
½ tsp	each salt and pepper
2	portobello mushrooms, stemmed and gills removed (see how-to, below)
1	red onion, cut in ½-inch (1 cm) thick rounds
1	zucchini, cut lengthwise in ¼-inch (5 mm) thick strips
4 cups	whole wheat rotini
2 cups	cherry tomatoes, halved
1	jar (175 mL) marinated artichoke hearts, drained and rinsed
⅓ cup	sliced pimiento-stuffed olives
¼ cup	shaved Parmesan cheese

HOW TO

STEM PORTOBELLO MUSHROOMS AND REMOVE GILLS

Cut stems off portobello mushrooms (or just trim off hard ends if stems are very short). Using spoon, scrape dark gills off undersides of caps. Discard gills and stems or save for making vegetable stock.

Makes 4 servings.

PER SERVING: about 613 cal, 21 g pro, 26 g total fat (4 g sat. fat), 83 g carb, 14 g fibre, 5 mg chol, 844 mg sodium. % RDI: 16% calcium, 32% iron, 19% vit A, 37% vit C, 35% folate.

MEDITERRANEAN FUSILLI SALAD

FRESH BASIL, HEARTY BEANS, SWEET SUN-DRIED TOMATOES AND AL DENTE PASTA MAKE THE PERFECT SUMMER SALAD. FUSILLI IS JUST THE RIGHT SHAPE; ITS CORKSCREW SPIRALS CATCH ALL THOSE YUMMY LITTLE TIDBITS OF VEGGIES AND HERBS, AND SOAK UP THE TASTY DRESSING.

172

INGREDIENTS

4 cups	fusilli pasta
1	zucchini, cubed
1	can (540 mL) romano beans, drained and rinsed
⅔ cup	sliced drained oil-packed sun-dried tomatoes
¾ cup	thinly sliced fresh basil

Cumin and Oregano Dressing:

⅔ cup	extra-virgin olive oil
¼ cup	red wine vinegar
1	clove garlic, minced
1 tsp	ground cumin
1 tsp	dried oregano
¼ tsp	each salt and pepper

METHOD

Cumin and Oregano Dressing: Whisk together oil, vinegar, garlic, cumin, oregano, salt and pepper; set aside.

In large pot of boiling salted water, cook pasta according to package directions until al dente. Drain and rinse under cold water; drain well. Place in large bowl.

Add zucchini, romano beans and sun-dried tomatoes; pour dressing over top. Toss to coat. (*Make-ahead: Cover and refrigerate for up to 24 hours.*)

Just before serving, toss with basil.

HOW TO

SUBSTITUTE DRY-PACKED SUN-DRIED TOMATOES

If you don't have a jar of oil-packed sun-dried tomatoes in your pantry, you can substitute the dry-packed type. Just soak them in boiling water until softened and pliable, about 15 minutes. Then drain, slice and add to recipes as directed. The soaked tomatoes will be a little chewier but just as sweet.

Makes 12 servings.

PER SERVING: about 263 cal, 6 g pro, 14 g total fat (2 g sat. fat), 30 g carb, 4 g fibre, 0 mg chol, 252 mg sodium. % RDI: 3% calcium, 16% iron, 3% vit A, 15% vit C, 41% folate.

TOMATO AND FETA ORZO SALAD
with lamb chops

THIS ALL-IN-ONE DISH IS LOVELY FOR A CASUAL DINNER PARTY WITH FRIENDS. GRILLING THE LAMB CHOPS GIVES THEM GREAT FLAVOUR, BUT WHEN THE WEATHER ISN'T COOPERATING, YOU CAN BROIL THE CHOPS INDOORS AND HAVE JUST AS MOUTHWATERING RESULTS.

174

INGREDIENTS

1	clove garlic
¼ tsp	salt
½ tsp	dried Italian herb seasoning
¼ tsp	pepper
8	lamb loin chops

Tomato and Feta Orzo Salad:

1 cup	orzo pasta
1½ cups	halved cherry tomatoes
⅓ cup	crumbled feta cheese
¼ cup	chopped fresh cilantro
¼ cup	finely diced red onion
2 tbsp	red wine vinegar
1 tbsp	extra-virgin olive oil
¼ tsp	each salt and pepper

METHOD

Tomato and Feta Orzo Salad: In saucepan of boiling salted water, cook orzo according to package directions. Drain well; transfer to bowl. Add tomatoes, feta cheese, cilantro, onion, vinegar, oil, salt and pepper; toss to coat. Set aside.

Meanwhile, finely chop garlic. Add salt; using flat side of chef's knife, rub into paste. Add Italian seasoning and pepper; rub all over lamb chops.

Place lamb on greased grill over medium-high heat; close lid and grill, turning once, until medium-rare, about 8 minutes. Serve with orzo salad.

Makes 4 servings.
PER SERVING: about 358 cal, 26 g pro, 12 g total fat (5 g sat. fat), 36 g carb, 3 g fibre, 80 mg chol, 575 mg sodium, 319 mg potassium. % RDI: 9% calcium, 17% iron, 7% vit A, 13% vit C, 10% folate.

LEMONY RED PEPPER AND ASPARAGUS PASTA SALAD

A SUNNY, CITRUSY VINAIGRETTE MAKES THIS PASTA SALAD EXCELLENT FOR A HOT SUMMER AFTERNOON.
THE ACIDITY OF THE DRESSING MELLOWS AS IT STANDS IN THE FRIDGE, SO THIS DISH IS EVEN BETTER THE NEXT DAY.

175

METHOD

In large pot of boiling lightly salted water, cook pasta according to package directions until al dente, adding asparagus during last 2 minutes of cooking. Drain and rinse under cold water; drain well. Transfer to large bowl.

Lemon Honey Dressing: In small bowl, whisk together lemon zest, lemon juice, honey, garlic, mustard, salt and pepper; slowly whisk in oil until emulsified.

Pour dressing over pasta mixture; add roasted red peppers and chives. Toss to combine. Cover and refrigerate for 6 hours. *(Make-ahead: Refrigerate for up to 24 hours.)*

HOW TO

TRIM ASPARAGUS AND PREP FOR COOKING

You can use a knife to trim off the tough, woody ends of asparagus spears, but it's much easier to just snap them off. Hold an asparagus spear at the woody end and halfway up the stalk, and bend until the end snaps off. If you don't like wasting the ends, use them to make asparagus soup; you'll need to purée and strain it to remove the fibrous bits.

INGREDIENTS

6 cups	farfalle pasta
1	bunch (450 g) asparagus, trimmed (see how-to, below) and cut in 1½-inch (4 cm) pieces
1	jar (370 mL) roasted red peppers, drained and sliced
½ cup	chopped fresh chives or sliced green onions

Lemon Honey Dressing:

1 tbsp	grated lemon zest
¼ cup	lemon juice
2 tsp	liquid honey
1	clove garlic, grated or pressed
1 tsp	Dijon mustard
¾ tsp	salt
¼ tsp	pepper
⅓ cup	olive oil

Makes 10 to 12 servings.
PER EACH OF 12 SERVINGS: about 209 cal, 6 g pro, 7 g total fat (1 g sat. fat), 32 g carb, 3 g fibre, 0 mg chol, 386 mg sodium, 136 mg potassium. % RDI: 2% calcium, 13% iron, 9% vit A, 62% vit C, 55% folate.

TUNA PASTA SALAD

USING TUNA PACKED IN A COMBINATION OF OIL AND BROTH MEANS YOU'LL NEED LESS OIL IN THE DRESSING. LOOK FOR ITALIAN OR SPANISH BRANDS—THEY PROVIDE THE RICHEST-TASTING FISH.

177

METHOD

Cut carrot in half lengthwise; cut carrot and celery into 4-inch (10 cm) lengths. In large pot of boiling salted water, cook carrot until tender-crisp, about 4 minutes. Using slotted spoon, remove from water; let cool. Add celery to pot; cook for 30 seconds. Using slotted spoon, remove from water; let cool. Thinly slice carrot and celery; set aside.

In same pot of boiling water, cook pasta according to package directions until al dente. Drain and rinse under cold water; drain well. Set aside.

In large bowl, break tuna into chunks; add pasta, carrot, celery, peas, pickles and onion.

Lemon Dijon Dressing: Whisk together lemon juice, vinegar, garlic, mustard, salt and pepper; slowly whisk in oil until emulsified. Add to pasta mixture; toss to coat. Cover and refrigerate for 4 hours. (*Make-ahead: Refrigerate for up to 2 days.*)

INGREDIENTS

1	large carrot
2	ribs celery
3 cups	medium shell pasta
2	cans (each 170 g) tuna packed in vegetable broth and oil, drained
½ cup	frozen peas, cooked and cooled
½ cup	chopped dill pickles
¼ cup	diced red onion

Lemon Dijon Dressing:

3 tbsp	lemon juice
3 tbsp	white wine vinegar
1	small clove garlic, minced
1 tsp	Dijon mustard
Pinch	each salt and pepper
¼ cup	extra-virgin olive oil

HOW TO

SOFTEN THE FLAVOUR OF RAW ONION

Onions can be potent, especially when they're added raw to salads. To make them milder, soak slices or pieces in cold water for 30 minutes. Drain well and add to salad as directed.

Makes 6 to 8 servings.

PER EACH OF 8 SERVINGS: about 234 cal, 13 g pro, 8 g total fat (1 g sat. fat), 27 g carb, 2 g fibre, 15 mg chol, 358 mg sodium. % RDI: 2% calcium, 12% iron, 21% vit A, 8% vit C, 33% folate.

SALMON PASTA SALAD

THIS SPEEDY SUPPER IS READY IN THE TIME IT TAKES TO COOK THE PASTA. MASHING THE BONES
IN WITH THE SALMON ADDS MORE CALCIUM. YOU CAN PICK THE BONES OUT IF YOU LIKE,
BUT WHEN THEY'RE MASHED, THEY'RE NOT NOTICEABLE IN THE FINAL DISH.

INGREDIENTS

4 cups	small shell pasta
1 cup	frozen peas
1	can (213 g) sockeye salmon, drained
½ cup	low-fat plain yogurt
⅓ cup	finely diced red onion
¼ cup	light mayonnaise
6	radishes, thinly sliced
2 tbsp	chopped fresh dill
½ tsp	each salt and pepper
½ tsp	hot pepper sauce
12	leaves romaine lettuce

METHOD

In large saucepan of boiling salted water, cook pasta according to package directions until al dente, adding peas in last 1 minute of cooking. Drain and rinse under cold water; drain well, shaking to remove excess water from insides of shells.

Meanwhile, flake salmon with fork, mashing in any bones; remove skin, if desired. Set aside.

In large bowl, stir together yogurt, onion, mayonnaise, radishes, dill, salt, pepper and hot pepper sauce.

Tear four of the lettuce leaves into bite-size pieces; add to dressing along with pasta mixture and salmon. Toss to combine.

Line four plates with remaining lettuce leaves; spoon salad onto lettuce.

Makes 4 servings.

PER SERVING: about 484 cal, 24 g pro, 10 g total fat (2 g sat. fat), 74 g carb, 6 g fibre, 26 mg chol, 985 mg sodium. % RDI: 18% calcium, 24% iron, 13% vit A, 25% vit C, 87% folate.

GRILLED VEGETABLE AND ISRAELI COUSCOUS SALAD

ISRAELI COUSCOUS IS MUCH LARGER AND MORE PASTA-LIKE THAN INSTANT COUSCOUS.
IF YOU CAN'T FIND IT, USE A SMALL ITALIAN PASTA, SUCH AS ORZO, DITALINI, ACINI DI PEPE OR SMALL SHELLS.

179

METHOD

In saucepan of boiling salted water, cook couscous according to package directions. Drain and rinse under cold water; drain well. Transfer to large bowl.

Meanwhile, slice eggplant; in colander, toss with ¼ tsp of the salt. Let drain for 10 minutes. Pat dry with paper towel.

Meanwhile, slice zucchini lengthwise. Slice red onion crosswise into ½-inch (1 cm) thick rounds.

Finely chop garlic. Add a pinch of the remaining salt; using flat side of chef's knife, rub into paste. Stir together garlic paste, oil, vinegar, sugar, pepper and remaining salt. Lightly brush some over eggplant, zucchini, onion and mushrooms.

Place vegetables on greased grill over medium heat; close lid and grill, turning often, until tender, 7 to 10 minutes. Cut into 1-inch (2.5 cm) pieces; add to couscous.

Add remaining oil mixture and parsley to couscous mixture; toss to coat. Let stand for 1 hour. *(Make-ahead: Refrigerate for up to 24 hours.)*

INGREDIENTS

2 cups	Israeli couscous
1	eggplant
1¼ tsp	salt
2	zucchini
1	small red onion
2	cloves garlic
½ cup	extra-virgin olive oil
¼ cup	sherry vinegar
¼ tsp	granulated sugar
¼ tsp	pepper
3	portobello mushrooms, stemmed and gills removed (see how-to, page 171)
⅓ cup	chopped fresh parsley

Makes 12 servings.
PER SERVING: about 212 cal, 5 g pro, 10 g total fat (1 g sat. fat), 27 g carb, 3 g fibre, 0 mg chol, 226 mg sodium, 346 mg potassium. % RDI: 2% calcium, 6% iron, 5% vit A, 8% vit C, 15% folate.

ITALIAN ORZO SALAD
with sausage, fennel and pepper skewers

THIS IS ANOTHER PASTA SALAD THAT'S DRESSED UP AND READY FOR COMPANY. THE SKEWERS ARE SO SIMPLE BUT
SUCH A NICE COMPLEMENT TO THE TENDER ORZO. IF THERE'S NO ORZO IN YOUR CUPBOARD,
CHOOSE A DIFFERENT PASTA SHAPE THAT'S ROUGHLY THE SAME SIZE.

INGREDIENTS

1	each small sweet red and green pepper
Half	bulb fennel, cored
4	mild or hot Italian sausages, cut in quarters

Orzo Salad:

1¼ cups	orzo or other small pasta
2 tbsp	extra-virgin olive oil
2 cups	cherry or grape tomatoes, halved
2	cloves garlic, minced
¼ tsp	dried oregano
Pinch	each salt and pepper
2 tbsp	minced fresh parsley
2 tbsp	balsamic vinegar
4 tsp	pesto

METHOD

Cut red and green peppers, and fennel into 2-inch (5 cm) chunks. Alternately thread vegetables and sausage onto each of four metal or soaked wooden skewers.

Place on greased grill over medium-high heat; close lid and grill, turning three times, until vegetables are tender and sausage is no longer pink inside, about 15 minutes.

Orzo Salad: Meanwhile, in saucepan of boiling salted water, cook orzo according to package directions. Drain; set aside.

Add oil to pan; heat over medium-high heat. Sauté tomatoes, garlic, oregano, salt and pepper until tomatoes are softened, about 3 minutes. Stir in parsley, vinegar and pesto. Add orzo; toss to coat. Serve with skewers.

TEST KITCHEN TIP

Soak wooden or bamboo skewers for 30 minutes in cold water before placing on the grill. This will keep the ends from charring and breaking off as you slip the food off them. Alternatively, you can wrap the tips of the skewers tightly in foil to keep them from blackening.

Makes 4 servings.
PER SERVING: about 508 cal, 23 g pro, 24 g total fat (6 g sat. fat), 50 g carb, 5 g fibre, 42 mg chol, 710 mg sodium. % RDI: 6% calcium, 19% iron, 16% vit A, 98% vit C, 15% folate.

GRILLED SAUSAGE, PEPPER AND BOCCONCINI PASTA SALAD

LITTLE NUGGETS OF CREAMY FRESH MOZZARELLA MAKE THIS PASTA SALAD TO-DIE-FOR DELISH. WE RECOMMEND HOT ITALIAN SAUSAGES, BUT MILD ARE TASTY IF YOU'RE NOT INTO SPICY FOODS.

METHOD

In saucepan of boiling salted water, cook pasta according to package directions. Drain and rinse under cold water; drain well. Set aside.

Meanwhile, finely chop garlic. Add salt; using flat side of chef's knife, rub into paste. In large bowl, whisk together garlic paste, oil, vinegar and pepper. Set aside.

Place sausages and red, yellow and green peppers on greased grill over medium heat; close lid and grill, turning often, until juices run clear when sausages are pierced and peppers are charred all over, 10 to 15 minutes.

Cut sausages into bite-size pieces; set aside. Peel, quarter and seed peppers; slice and add to dressing. Toss to coat.

Cut radicchio in half lengthwise; remove core. Grill, turning often, until leaves are tender and slightly charred, about 5 minutes. Transfer to cutting board; slice. Add to pepper mixture along with pasta, sausage, bocconcini cheese and basil; toss to coat.

INGREDIENTS

3 cups	penne pasta
1	large clove garlic
¼ tsp	salt
¼ cup	extra-virgin olive oil
3 tbsp	red wine vinegar
¼ tsp	pepper
4	hot or mild Italian sausages
1	each sweet red, yellow and green pepper
1	head radicchio
1	tub (200 g) small bocconcini cheese, drained
¼ cup	loosely packed fresh basil leaves, thinly sliced

Makes 4 servings.

PER SERVING: about 726 cal, 35 g pro, 40 g total fat (14 g sat. fat), 57 g carb, 5 g fibre, 81 mg chol, 1,166 mg sodium, 508 mg potassium. % RDI: 32% calcium, 31% iron, 23% vit A, 197% vit C, 76% folate.

JAPANESE NOODLE SALAD

YOU DON'T OFTEN SEE COMPOSED NOODLE SALADS IN NORTH AMERICA, BUT THIS ONE IS A SUMMERTIME STAPLE IN JAPAN, WHEN COOKS ARE TRYING TO BEAT THE HEAT. OTHER TOPPINGS CAN BE LOVELY ON THIS SALAD TOO: TRY LIGHTLY BLANCHED JULIENNED CARROT OR BABY SPINACH IF YOU LIKE.

184

INGREDIENTS

1	pkg (340 g) chuka soba noodles or ramen noodles
2	eggs
1	green onion (dark green part only)
1 tsp	vegetable oil
1 cup	shredded romaine lettuce
Half	English cucumber, julienned (see how-to, page 36)
2	plum tomatoes, quartered
1 tbsp	toasted sesame seeds

Sesame Shiitake Dressing:

1	pkg (7 g) dried shiitake mushrooms
1 cup	boiling water
3 tbsp	unseasoned rice vinegar
2 tbsp	soy sauce
4 tsp	granulated sugar
1 tsp	sesame oil

METHOD

Sesame Shiitake Dressing: In glass measure, soak mushrooms in boiling water until softened, about 10 minutes. Reserving liquid, remove mushrooms and pat dry; thinly slice. Strain liquid into small bowl; add vinegar, soy sauce, sugar and sesame oil. Set aside.

Meanwhile, cook noodles according to package directions. Drain and rinse under cold water; drain well. Pat dry.

In small bowl, beat eggs with 1 tsp water; stir in green onion. In nonstick skillet, heat oil over medium-low heat; pour in egg mixture and cook, without stirring, to make thin omelette. Transfer to cutting board; thinly slice.

Divide noodles among four plates. Surround with piles of lettuce, cucumber, tomatoes, eggs and mushrooms. Sprinkle with sesame seeds. Serve each plate with small dish of dressing to pour over top.

TEST KITCHEN TIP

If you like ginger, garnish with red beni shoga, a pungent shredded pickled ginger that's dyed bright red. If you can't find it in an Asian grocery store, try a bit of pink or natural sushi ginger instead.

Makes 4 servings.

PER SERVING: about 399 cal, 20 g pro, 6 g total fat (1 g sat. fat), 73 g carb, 5 g fibre, 93 mg chol, 949 mg sodium. % RDI: 4% calcium, 18% iron, 7% vit A, 10% vit C, 25% folate.

KOREAN COLD SOMEN NOODLE SALAD

THIS SALAD IS A REFRESHING TAKE ON THE COLD NOODLE SALADS THAT ARE POPULAR FARE DURING HOT KOREAN SUMMERS. TO GET KIMCHI JUICE, GENTLY SQUEEZE THE KIMCHI AND TOP UP WITH SOME OF THE BRINE FROM THE JAR.

187

METHOD

Pickled Daikon: Combine daikon, vinegar and sugar; refrigerate for 15 minutes.

Meanwhile, in large pot of boiling water, cook noodles according to package directions. Drain and rinse under cold running water until no longer starchy. Drain well; shake to remove excess water. Set aside to dry for 10 minutes.

Sauce: Meanwhile, stir together hot pepper paste, vinegar, sesame seeds, sesame oil, sugar and soy sauce; set aside.

In bowl, combine noodles, cucumber, ham (if using), pear, kimchi, green onion and kimchi juice; add half of the sauce and toss to combine.

Add frisée, tossing gently; sprinkle with nori. Divide among bowls; top with pickled daikon. Serve remaining sauce on the side.

TEST KITCHEN TIP

This salad requires a trip to a grocery store that stocks Korean ingredients specifically. Korean hot pepper paste (gochujang) has a distinctive taste this salad requires; there will be a large selection of it in tubs, ranging in size from small to giant. While you're at the store, pick up the kimchi; there are dozens of varieties, but you'll need straight-up cabbage kimchi for this recipe.

INGREDIENTS

275 g	somen noodles
Half	English cucumber, halved lengthwise, cored and sliced
125 g	deli sliced ham (optional), julienned
1½ cups	sliced cored Asian pear
1 cup	kimchi, chopped
½ cup	finely chopped green onion
¼ cup	kimchi juice
4 cups	shredded frisée or red leaf lettuce
1	sheet roasted nori, cut in strips

Sauce:

3 tbsp	Korean hot pepper paste (gochujang)
3 tbsp	unseasoned rice vinegar
2 tbsp	toasted sesame seeds
2 tbsp	sesame oil
4 tsp	granulated sugar
1 tbsp	sodium-reduced soy sauce

Pickled Daikon:

½ cup	thinly sliced peeled daikon
1 tbsp	unseasoned rice vinegar
½ tsp	granulated sugar

Makes 4 to 6 servings.

PER EACH OF 6 SERVINGS: about 257 cal, 6 g pro, 7 g total fat (I g sat. fat), 43 g carb, 6 g fibre, 0 mg chol, 908 mg sodium, 269 mg potassium. % RDI: 4% calcium, 12% iron, 22% vit A, 23% vit C, 30% folate.

Cold Salads:
How to Stay Safe Outdoors

Hot weather and cold salads aren't an ideal match, but these tips will help keep you safe.

In Canada, tens of thousands of cases of foodborne illness (better known as food poisoning) are reported every year—and plenty more go undocumented. The culprits are usually bacteria, such as E. coli and salmonella, lurking in all sorts of places. Cold salads (usually the ones that contain eggs, poultry, meat or fish), and raw veggies and fruit are often high on the list of suspects.

Add a few hot, humid days and a couple of lazy picnic lunches and you have a definite recipe for food poisoning, especially in the summer. Here are some safe handling practices you can use to keep your salads (and more) safe.

- Wash fruits and vegetables well before eating or adding to recipes. If you have a clean vegetable brush, use it to scrub the rinds or skins to remove as much surface bacteria as possible. Whatever you don't remove can end up on the inside when you cut through the outside.

- Plan amounts carefully to avoid leftovers; if you are unable to refrigerate them right away, discard any uneaten meat, poultry, seafood, salads or dairy products when the meal is done.

- Cold foods should stay that way. The optimal range for storage is below 40°F (4°C). The danger zone between 60 and 80°F (16 and 27°C) is where dangerous bacteria multiply like lightning. Perishable foods should stay chilled up to the last moment before serving.

- Keep serving times outdoors as short as possible. Chill food before packing, and always keep your food covered and chilled inside coolers well stocked with ice and ice packs. Place coolers in the shade for as long as possible if you're picnicking in a sunny location. Don't let any dishes stand out for more than two hours; even less if the day is sunny and hot.

- The storage life of a pasta salad is only as long as the life of the most perishable ingredient in it: that's two days max for seafood, and only two or three days for chicken.

- There may not be clean water and soap available at your picnic area or campground. Pack travel wipes, hand sanitizer and paper towels so you can clean your hands and any surfaces easily.

THAI BEEF NOODLE SALAD

THIS SALAD COMBINES ALL THE MAIN THAI TASTES—SOUR, SALTY, HOT AND SWEET—IN ONE PERFECT MEAL. LOOK FOR TINY BUT FIERY THAI BIRD'S-EYE PEPPERS IN THE PRODUCE AISLE OR AT YOUR LOCAL ASIAN GROCERY STORE. SERRANO PEPPERS WORK WELL TOO, AND OFFER A COMPARABLE AMOUNT OF SPICY HEAT.

METHOD

Marinade: In glass baking dish, combine ginger, soy sauce, garlic, sugar, sesame oil and vegetable oil; add steak, turning to coat. Cover and refrigerate for 4 hours, turning occasionally. *(Make-ahead: Refrigerate for up to 12 hours.)*

Dressing: In jar with tight-fitting lid, shake hot water with sugar until dissolved. Add lime juice, fish sauce and Thai peppers; shake to combine. *(Make-ahead: Refrigerate for up to 5 days.)*

Using vegetable peeler, slice cucumber lengthwise into thin strips, slicing around and discarding centre seeds; set aside. Slice carrot lengthwise into thin strips; set aside.

In large pot of boiling salted water, cook rice noodles according to package directions. Drain and rinse under cold water; drain well. In large bowl, toss noodles with dressing; set aside.

Discarding marinade, place steak on greased grill over medium-high heat; close lid and grill, turning once, until medium-rare, about 8 minutes. Transfer to cutting board and tent with foil; let stand for 5 minutes before thinly slicing across the grain.

Add cucumber, carrot, red onion, cilantro, mint and basil to noodle mixture; toss to coat. Divide among bowls or plates; top with steak. Sprinkle with peanuts.

INGREDIENTS

1	beef flank marinating steak (about 450 g)
1	piece (8 inches/20 cm long) English cucumber
1	large carrot
175 g	rice stick noodles (about ⅓ inch/ 8 mm) wide
Quarter	red onion, thinly sliced
3 tbsp	each chopped fresh cilantro and mint
3 tbsp	Thai or other basil leaves
¼ cup	chopped unsalted peanuts

Marinade:

2 tbsp	grated fresh ginger
2 tbsp	soy sauce
2	cloves garlic, minced
1 tbsp	granulated sugar
1 tbsp	each sesame oil and vegetable oil

Dressing:

½ cup	hot water
¼ cup	granulated sugar
2 tbsp	lime juice
2 tbsp	fish sauce
2	Thai bird's-eye peppers or serrano chilies, seeded and thinly sliced

Makes 4 to 6 servings.

PER EACH OF 6 SERVINGS: about 363 cal, 21 g pro, 13 g total fat (3 g sat. fat), 41 g carb, 3 g fibre, 31 mg chol, 873 mg sodium. % RDI: 4% calcium, 15% iron, 26% vit A, 20% vit C, 14% folate.

RICE VERMICELLI SALAD
with vietnamese pork chops

THIS SALAD IS AS GOOD AS ANY YOU'LL FIND IN A VIETNAMESE RESTAURANT.
IT TAKES A FAIR BIT OF CHOPPING AND PREPARATION, BUT IT'S WELL WORTH THE WORK.

METHOD

Vietnamese Pork Chops: In bowl, whisk together shallots, brown sugar, lime juice, fish sauce, oil and pepper; add pork, turning to coat. Cover and marinate for 15 minutes. Pour marinade into small saucepan; set aside.

Place pork on greased grill over medium-high heat; close lid and grill, turning once, until juices run clear when pork is pierced and just a hint of pink remains inside, about 10 minutes. Transfer to plate; tent with foil. Let stand for 5 minutes before thinly slicing.

Dressing: Meanwhile, stir together lime juice, sugar, boiling water, fish sauce, garlic and hot pepper. Set aside.

In large bowl, soak rice vermicelli according to package directions. Drain and rinse under cold water; drain well, squeezing out excess water. Return vermicelli to bowl; add dressing, lettuce, carrot, mint and cilantro. Toss to coat.

Meanwhile, bring reserved marinade to boil over high heat; reduce heat and simmer until syrupy, 4 to 5 minutes.

Arrange salad on four plates; top with pork. Sprinkle with peanuts (if using); serve with sauce.

INGREDIENTS

125 g	rice stick vermicelli
2 cups	shredded leaf lettuce
½ cup	finely grated carrot
¼ cup	each shredded fresh mint and cilantro
¼ cup	chopped roasted peanuts (optional)

Vietnamese Pork Chops:

½ cup	finely chopped shallots or onion
3 tbsp	packed brown sugar
2 tbsp	each lime juice and fish sauce
1 tbsp	vegetable oil
½ tsp	pepper
4	boneless pork loin centre chops, trimmed

Dressing:

3 tbsp	lime juice
1 tbsp	granulated sugar
1 tbsp	boiling water
1 tbsp	fish sauce
1	clove garlic, minced
½ tsp	minced hot pepper

Makes 4 servings.

PER SERVING: about 346 cal, 24 g pro, 6 g total fat (1 g sat. fat), 47 g carb, 3 g fibre, 45 mg chol, 812 mg sodium, 540 mg potassium. % RDI: 5% calcium, 15% iron, 42% vit A, 17% vit C, 18% folate.

PUTTANESCA POTATO SALAD

**HERE, TWO FAVOURITE DISHES—RICH PUTTANESCA PASTA AND COMFORTING POTATO SALAD—
SHARE THEIR BEST QUALITIES AND BECOME A CREATIVE SIDE DISH. THIS IS A TERRIFIC RECIPE FOR SHOWING
OFF A SPECIAL FRUITY OLIVE OIL YOU'VE BEEN SAVING.**

192

INGREDIENTS

1.35 kg	mini red-skinned potatoes, scrubbed and quartered
⅓ cup	extra-virgin olive oil
1 cup	finely chopped onion
3	cloves garlic, minced
1 tsp	hot pepper flakes
½ tsp	dried oregano
4	anchovy fillets, finely chopped (see tip, page 37)
½ cup	thinly sliced drained oil-packed sun-dried tomatoes
½ cup	chopped oil-cured olives
3 tbsp	capers, drained, rinsed and chopped
⅓ cup	white wine vinegar
⅓ cup	chopped fresh parsley

METHOD

In large pot of boiling salted water, cook potatoes until fork-tender, about 10 minutes. Drain; place in large bowl.

Meanwhile, in large skillet, heat oil over medium heat; cook onion until golden, about 8 minutes.

Stir in garlic, hot pepper flakes, oregano and anchovies; cook, stirring, until fragrant and garlic is browned. Stir in sun-dried tomatoes, olives and capers; cook for 1 minute. Stir in vinegar until heated through, scraping up browned bits from bottom of pan.

Pour over potatoes. Add parsley; toss to coat. Cover and refrigerate for 2 hours. (*Make-ahead: Refrigerate for up to 24 hours.*)

Makes 12 servings.

PER SERVING: about 176 cal, 3 g pro, 9 g total fat (1 g sat. fat), 22 g carb, 3 g fibre, 1 mg chol, 542 mg sodium, 584 mg potassium. % RDI: 3% calcium, 10% iron, 3% vit A, 40% vit C, 10% folate.

SMASHED POTATO SALAD

THIS RECIPE CREATES A CLASSIC CREAMY POTATO SALAD; KEEP IT ON HAND FOR BARBECUES, PICNICS AND POTLUCKS. BOTH SWEET AND SOUR GHERKINS WORK WELL, SO CHOOSE WHICHEVER SUITS YOUR PALATE.

METHOD

In large pot of boiling salted water, cook potatoes until fork-tender, about 15 minutes. Drain and coarsely chop; place in large bowl.

Add eggs, onion, celery and pickles to potatoes, breaking up slightly with potato masher.

Whisk together mayonnaise, mustard, vinegar, salt, pepper and paprika. Add to potatoes; mix well. Cover and refrigerate until chilled, about 1 hour. (*Make-ahead: Refrigerate for up to 24 hours.*)

INGREDIENTS

4	large white potatoes (about 750 g), peeled
3	hard-cooked eggs (see how-to, page 79), chopped
Half	Vidalia or other sweet onion, finely chopped
2	ribs celery, diced
½ cup	diced gherkin pickles
½ cup	mayonnaise
2 tbsp	Dijon mustard
1 tbsp	cider vinegar
¾ tsp	salt
½ tsp	pepper
¼ tsp	sweet paprika

**PHOTO
PAGE 195**

Makes 8 servings.
PER SERVING: about 208 cal, 4 g pro, 13 g total fat (2 g sat. fat), 20 g carb, 2 g fibre, 75 mg chol, 634 mg sodium, 315 mg potassium. % RDI: 3% calcium, 6% iron, 5% vit A, 12% vit C, 11% folate.

COLESLAW
with cider vinaigrette

PAGE 211

SMASHED
POTATO SALAD

PAGE 193

ROASTED TWO-POTATO SALAD

ONE POTATO, TWO POTATO, THREE POTATO, FOUR. IF YOU REALLY LIKE THIS, YOU CAN HAVE SOME MORE!
THE BACON IS OPTIONAL, BUT IT ADDS A SMOKY DIMENSION TO THE SALAD THAT
REALLY COMPLEMENTS BOTH THE SWEET AND YELLOW POTATOES.

INGREDIENTS

900 g	yellow-fleshed potatoes
675 g	sweet potatoes
⅓ cup	extra-virgin olive oil
½ tsp	dried thyme
½ tsp	each salt and pepper
4	slices bacon (optional)
¼ cup	chopped fresh parsley
2 tbsp	lemon juice
1 tbsp	Dijon mustard
½ tsp	hot pepper sauce
4	green onions, sliced

METHOD

Peel yellow-fleshed and sweet potatoes; cut into 1-inch (2.5 cm) cubes. In large bowl, toss together potatoes, ¼ cup of the oil, thyme, salt and pepper.

Spread potatoes in large shallow roasting pan; roast in 375°F (190°C) oven, turning once, until tender and golden, about 40 minutes. Let stand for 5 minutes. Transfer to large bowl.

Meanwhile, in skillet, cook bacon (if using) over medium heat, turning once, until crisp, about 5 minutes. Drain on paper towel–lined plate; chop.

Stir together parsley, lemon juice, mustard, hot pepper sauce, green onions, bacon (if using) and remaining oil. Add to potatoes; toss to coat. (*Make-ahead: Cover and refrigerate for up to 24 hours. Serve at room temperature.*)

Makes 8 servings.

PER SERVING: about 216 cal, 3 g pro, 9 g total fat (1 g sat. fat), 31 g carb, 4 g fibre, 0 mg chol, 200 mg sodium, 718 mg potassium. % RDI: 4% calcium, 12% iron, 120% vit A, 45% vit C, 9% folate.

WARM POTATO SALAD WITH CHORIZO

SAVOURY, SLIGHTLY SPICY CHORIZO SAUSAGE TURNS REGULAR POTATO SALAD INTO A MEAL.
IT'S AN INTERESTING TWIST THAT'S FANCY ENOUGH FOR ENTERTAINING, AND IT
MAKES A SENSATIONAL ADDITION TO A BARBECUE MENU.

197

METHOD

In large pot of boiling salted water, cook potatoes until fork-tender, 20 to 25 minutes. Drain; let cool enough to handle. Cut into thick slices; transfer to large bowl.

Meanwhile, in separate saucepan, cover eggs with enough cold water to cover by 1 inch (2.5 cm); bring to boil. Remove from heat; cover and let stand for 12 minutes. Drain and chill under cold water. Drain, peel off shells and thinly slice; add to potatoes.

Meanwhile, in large skillet, heat oil over medium heat; cook chorizo, stirring occasionally, until browned, 3 to 4 minutes. Using slotted spoon, add to potatoes.

Add onion to pan; cook, stirring occasionally, until golden, 6 to 8 minutes. Add broth and vinegar; bring to boil. Pour over potato mixture. Add green onions, mustard, salt and pepper; toss gently to coat.

INGREDIENTS

900 g	yellow-fleshed potatoes, scrubbed
3	eggs
2 tbsp	olive oil
1	dry-cured chorizo sausage, sliced
1	onion, diced
¾ cup	vegetable broth
¼ cup	white wine vinegar
½ cup	chopped green onions
2 tbsp	grainy mustard
¼ tsp	each salt and pepper

TEST KITCHEN TIP

There are two types of chorizo to look out for. Dry-cured, from Spain and Portugal, doesn't have to be cooked before eating (although browning slices gives them a fabulous crispy finish). It can be added to recipes or eaten as is like other charcuterie. Fresh chorizo, from South America, contains raw meat, is milder than dry-cured chorizo and must be cooked before eating. The two types aren't interchangeable in recipes.

Makes 4 servings.

PER SERVING: about 376 cal, 13 g pro, 17 g total fat (4 g sat. fat), 43 g carb, 4 g fibre, 176 mg chol, 1,076 mg sodium, 917 mg potassium. % RDI: 6% calcium, 20% iron, 8% vit A, 42% vit C, 21% folate.

Perfect Potatoes for Salads

So which of these tasty tubers is right for everyone's favourite picnic side dish? Here's what you need to know about different varieties and how to store your spuds.

BOILING VS. BAKING POTATOES

Boiling potatoes, such as white potatoes, have a waxy texture when cooked, which helps them hold their shape. They're the right texture for salads like the ones in this chapter. Baking potatoes, such as russet potatoes, have a floury, or fluffy, texture that makes them better for baking, mashing and frying. All-purpose yellow-fleshed potatoes, commonly found in the produce aisle at the supermarket, can typically be substituted for either category.

BUYING

Your eyes and your nose are the best tools for choosing potatoes. They should smell neutral like soil—avoid any that have an off odour. Select potatoes with smooth, unblemished skins. Avoid discoloured or mouldy ones or any that have begun to sprout.

Do not buy potatoes with green-tinged skin. This indicates the presence of the toxin solanine, which develops when potatoes are exposed to light (a common occurrence with potatoes sold in clear plastic bags rather than dark paper ones). Since the green part is just an indicator of solanine (not the compound itself), it's not advisable to try to cut those areas away. It's best to throw out the potatoes and buy fresh ones.

STORING

If you have purchased potatoes in plastic bags, remove them as soon as you get home. Store the potatoes, unwashed, in an open storage rack or basket, or a well-aerated bin in a cool, dark, dry place. An area with an average temperature of 44 to 50°F (7 to 10°C) with good air circulation is ideal.

Exposing potatoes to lower temperatures or putting them in the refrigerator causes decay and darkening. The cold gives them a woody texture and converts their starch to sugar, making them taste disagreeably sweet.

Higher temperatures aren't any better. When potatoes are kept at temperatures above 50°F (10°C), they may start to sprout, become flabby or rot. Storing potatoes with onions also hastens their deterioration.

Even minimal exposure to light can make potatoes turn green and sprout. If you don't have a cool basement or storage area, store potatoes loosely packed in a paper sack in a dark cupboard next to an outside wall.

New potatoes should be kept for only about one week, so buy them in small quantities. Mature potatoes will stay fresh for several weeks if stored properly.

FULLY LOADED POTATO SALAD

THIS MOUTHWATERING SALAD CONJURES UP MEMORIES OF THE MOST SCRUMPTIOUS STUFFED BAKED POTATO YOU'VE EVER TASTED. IF YOU DON'T HAVE ANY FRESH CHIVES ON HAND, YOU CAN USE VERY THINLY SLICED GREEN ONIONS FOR A SLIGHTLY MORE ASSERTIVE GARNISH.

METHOD

In large pot of boiling salted water, cook potatoes until tender, about 25 minutes. Drain and let cool slightly; peel. Refrigerate until completely cool; cut into chunks.

In large bowl, stir together sour cream, mayonnaise, salt and pepper. Add potatoes; toss to coat. Add cheese; gently toss to combine. *(Make-ahead: Cover and refrigerate for up to 24 hours.)*

Meanwhile, in large skillet, cook bacon over medium heat, turning once, until crisp, about 8 minutes. Drain on paper towel–lined plate; let cool slightly. Chop.

To serve, sprinkle bacon and chives over salad.

INGREDIENTS

1.5 kg	white potatoes (about 7), scrubbed
1 cup	light sour cream
¾ cup	light mayonnaise
½ tsp	each salt and pepper
¾ cup	crumbled blue cheese
4	slices thick-cut bacon
3 tbsp	chopped fresh chives

PHOTO
PAGE 147

Makes 6 to 8 servings.

PER EACH OF 8 SERVINGS: about 305 cal, 9 g pro, 14 g total fat (5 g sat. fat), 36 g carb, 2 g fibre, 26 mg chol, 951 mg sodium, 718 mg potassium. % RDI: 12% calcium, 5% iron, 5% vit A, 33% vit C, 10% folate.

POTATO PERSILLADE SALAD

PERSILLADE, A FRENCH SAUCE MADE WITH FRESH PARSLEY AND GARLIC, PERKS UP THE FLAVOUR OF THESE POTATOES AND MAKE THIS AN EXTRAORDINARY TAKE ON A PLAIN-OLD PICNIC SIDE DISH. ORDINARY WHITE OR RED-SKINNED BOILING POTATOES GIVE THIS SALAD THE BEST TEXTURE.

200

INGREDIENTS

1.35 kg	potatoes, peeled
4	green onions, thinly sliced

Persillade Sauce:

1 cup	loosely packed fresh parsley leaves
⅓ cup	extra-virgin olive oil
1	clove garlic, minced
2 tbsp	lemon juice
½ tsp	each salt and pepper

METHOD

Persillade Sauce: In food processor, chop together parsley, oil, garlic, lemon juice, salt and pepper until almost smooth. Set aside.

In large pot of boiling salted water, cook potatoes until tender, 20 to 25 minutes. Drain; let cool slightly. Cut into chunks.

In bowl, toss potatoes with green onions. Pour sauce over top; toss to coat.

TEST KITCHEN TIP

Combine the persillade sauce with fresh bread crumbs to make a delicious topping for roast meats. Spread the mixture over the outside of a rack of lamb or a pork roast before sliding it into the oven, then enjoy the crisp, golden, flavourful crust it forms. Persillade also makes an excellent sauce for fish.

Makes 8 servings.

PER SERVING: about 203 cal, 3 g pro, 9 g total fat (1 g sat. fat), 29 g carb, 2 g fibre, 0 mg chol, 478 mg sodium. % RDI: 3% calcium, 8% iron, 7% vit A, 38% vit C, 13% folate.

POTATO AND CAULIFLOWER SALAD

CAULIFLOWER MAY NOT BE THE FIRST VEGETABLE YOU'D THINK TO ADD TO A SALAD,
BUT IT IS A TASTY PARTNER TO POTATOES. IT HAS A NICE BITE AND A MELLOW, EARTHY FLAVOUR
THAT GOES WELL WITH THE SALTY OLIVES AND SIMPLE VINAIGRETTE.

202

INGREDIENTS

4	large yellow-fleshed potatoes, scrubbed
Half	head cauliflower, cut in florets
2	ribs celery, diced
1 cup	oil-cured black olives, pitted

Parsley Vinaigrette:

⅓ cup	olive oil
3 tbsp	chopped fresh parsley
3 tbsp	red wine vinegar
½ tsp	salt

METHOD

In large pot of boiling salted water, cook potatoes until tender, 30 minutes. Drain, peel and cut into 1-inch (2.5 cm) cubes.

Meanwhile, in separate saucepan of boiling salted water, cook cauliflower until tender, about 4 minutes. Drain.

In large bowl, toss together potatoes, cauliflower, celery and black olives.

Parsley Vinaigrette: Stir together oil, parsley, vinegar and salt; toss with potato mixture to coat.

Makes 6 servings.

PER SERVING: about 300 cal, 4 g pro, 20 g total fat (3 g sat. fat), 28 g carb, 4 g fibre, 0 mg chol, 1,349 mg sodium, 573 mg potassium. % RDI: 4% calcium, 8% iron, 2% vit A, 65% vit C, 18% folate.

DILLED POTATO AND GRILLED CORN SALAD

GRILLED CORN HAS A SMOKY FLAVOUR AND A CARAMELIZED SWEETNESS THAT MAKES
IT A TASTY STAR IN ALL SORTS OF DISHES. HERE, IT PLAYS NICELY WITH DILL, POTATOES
AND GRAINY MUSTARD IN A RICHLY FLAVOURED LATE-SUMMER SIDE DISH.

203

METHOD

Brush corn with 1 tbsp of the oil. Place on greased grill over medium-high heat; close lid and grill until tender and slightly charred, 10 to 15 minutes. Let cool. Cut off kernels (see how-to, below); place in large bowl.

Meanwhile, in large saucepan of boiling salted water, cook potatoes until tender, about 15 minutes. Drain and halve; add to bowl with corn.

Add green onions, mustard, salt and pepper; sprinkle with vinegar. Toss well to combine. Let cool.

Add remaining oil and dill; toss to coat.

INGREDIENTS

4	cobs corn, husked
3 tbsp	vegetable oil
900 g	small red or white potatoes (about 30), peeled
4	green onions, sliced
2 tsp	grainy mustard
½ tsp	salt
¼ tsp	pepper
¼ cup	red wine vinegar
2 tbsp	chopped fresh dill

HOW TO

CUT FRESH CORN OFF THE COB

Trim the bottom end of the cob flat; place it on a cutting board, cut side down. Grasp the top of the cob firmly, near the point. Using a sharp knife and starting close to the top, cut downward, following the contour of the cob to remove the kernels. Use a gentle sawing motion to get the most out of the kernels. Break apart any clumps of cut corn.

Makes 6 to 8 servings.

PER EACH OF 8 SERVINGS: about 197 cal, 4 g pro, 6 g total fat (1 g sat. fat), 34 g carb,
4 g fibre, 0 mg chol, 400 mg sodium, 641 mg potassium. % RDI: 2% calcium, 10% iron,
2% vit A, 37% vit C, 22% folate.

All About Cabbage

Cabbage is cabbage, right? Nope! There are many kinds with different tastes and textures to recommend them. Here's what you need to know about this sturdy garden veg.

A NUTRITIONAL POWERHOUSE

Cabbage is a health-food superstar. It's a member of the cruciferous vegetable family, which includes kale, broccoli and cauliflower. It's a source of fibre, vitamins such as folate and vitamin C, and minerals such as potassium. The best part, though, is that it's full of cancer-fighting compounds, so it makes a very nutritious addition to your diet.

A VERSATILE INGREDIENT

Buying a whole head of cabbage may seem a little daunting. What are you going to do with all those leftovers after you've shredded a few cups for slaw? The answer: plenty! Cabbage is tasty raw in salads and slaws, and it takes on a sweet note when cooked, making it lovely in stir-fries, soups and stews. It's best cooked for short periods of time to preserve the nutrient content.

A LONG LIFE

Cabbage is very sturdy, so it's ideal for making keeper salads. The shredded leaves stay crisp and vibrant, even when they have been dressed for several days. They also don't mind the cold in the fridge, so you can make a slaw on Monday and serve it well into the middle of the week. Try leftover slaw on sandwiches as an alternative to lettuce or other veggies. (It's absolutely killer on a pulled pork sandwich.)

TYPES OF CABBAGE

- **Brussels sprouts** are just tiny cabbages, with a more aggressive cabbage flavour. They are fabulous served cooked as a side dish, but raw shredded brussels sprouts make tasty slaws (especially when paired with smoky bacon).
- **Green cabbage** is one of the most common types you'll find in the supermarket. Look for a head that is heavy for its size, with tightly packed leaves that are crisp and pale green. Green cabbage has a strong, vegetal, slightly sweet flavour.
- **Napa cabbage** is an Asian cabbage with a mild flavour. Its heads are long and cylindrical, with green leaves that fade into pale roots. It's a must-have for Asian-style salads and stir-fries.
- **Red cabbage** comes in compact, round heads, with tightly curled leaves. A good one will feel heavy and have shiny, deep purple-red leaves. It tastes like green cabbage, but adds its beautiful colour to dishes.
- **Savoy cabbage** is like a milder version of green cabbage, with wrinkled yellow-green leaves. Perfect heads are round, heavy and quite large, and the leaves are beautiful shredded in salads.

KOHLRABI AND RUTABAGA SLAW

KOHLRABI LOOKS A LITTLE LIKE AN ALIEN'S HEAD, BUT ITS RAW RADISH–CABBAGE FLAVOUR IS LOVELY IN SLAWS. DIDN'T KNOW YOU COULD ALSO EAT RUTABAGA RAW? YOU BET!

METHOD

In large bowl, whisk together mayonnaise, yogurt, lemon juice, mustard, salt and pepper.

Add kohlrabi, rutabaga and parsley; toss to coat. *(Make-ahead: Refrigerate in airtight container for up to 3 days. Toss before serving.)*

INGREDIENTS

¼ cup	light mayonnaise
¼ cup	Balkan-style plain yogurt
1 tbsp	lemon juice
2 tsp	Dijon mustard
¼ tsp	each salt and pepper
2 cups	julienned peeled trimmed kohlrabi (see how-to, page 36)
2 cups	julienned peeled rutabaga
¼ cup	chopped fresh parsley

TEST KITCHEN TIP

The simple dressing for this slaw is equally tasty over julienned peeled celeriac or broccoli stems, or shredded brussels sprouts.

Makes 4 to 6 servings.

PER EACH OF 6 SERVINGS: about 70 cal, 2 g pro, 4 g total fat (I g sat. fat), 8 g carb, 3 g fibre, 5 mg chol, 208 mg sodium, 325 mg potassium. % RDI: 5% calcium, 4% iron, 3% vit A, 63% vit C, 9% folate.

CABBAGE SALAD
with ginger dressing

ASIAN CUISINE OFTEN FEATURES SHREDDED CABBAGE, AND RAW SALADS ARE A COMMON WAY OF ENJOYING THIS NUTRITIOUS VEGETABLE. HERE IT PAIRS UP WITH A SENSATIONALLY TASTY (AND EASY!) GINGER DRESSING YOU'LL WANT TO EAT ON OTHER SALADS, TOO.

206

INGREDIENTS

4 cups	finely shredded napa cabbage
1 cup	julienned carrots (see how-to, page 36)

Ginger Dressing:

¼ cup	unseasoned rice vinegar
1 tbsp	soy sauce
1 tsp	granulated sugar
½ tsp	grated fresh ginger

METHOD

Ginger Dressing: Whisk together vinegar, soy sauce, sugar and ginger. Set aside.

In large bowl, toss cabbage with carrots; divide among four plates. Drizzle with dressing.

TEST KITCHEN TIP

Unseasoned rice vinegar is just vinegar made from rice (not rice wine, as is commonly assumed). Seasoned rice vinegar contains added salt and sugar; it's a shortcut ingredient often used for flavouring sushi rice. By using unseasoned rice vinegar in this and many other recipes, we're able to control and adjust the amount of salt and sugar in the dish.

Makes 4 servings.

PER SERVING: about 33 cal, 2 g pro, trace total fat (0 g sat. fat), 8 g carb, 2 g fibre, 0 mg chol, 254 mg sodium, 292 mg potassium. % RDI: 6% calcium, 3% iron, 53% vit A, 37% vit C, 30% folate.

CLASSIC COLESLAW

FRESH, CRISP AND TANGY, COLESLAW MAKES AN IDEAL SIDE DISH FOR FRIED FISH
AND BARBECUED MAINS. THE EXTRA STEP OF DRAINING THE SHREDDED CABBAGE HELPS
THE COLESLAW KEEP FOR A LONGER PERIOD WITHOUT GETTING WATERY.

METHOD

In large bowl, toss cabbage with 1 tsp of the salt. In separate
bowl, toss together carrots, red onion and remaining salt.
Let both stand for 1 hour.

In colander, drain cabbage. One handful at a time, squeeze out
excess moisture; return cabbage to bowl. Add carrots, onion and
accumulated juices; toss to combine.

Whisk together vinegar, oil, sugar, mustard and celery seeds;
pour over cabbage mixture. Add parsley; toss to coat. Cover and
refrigerate for 1 hour. *(Make-ahead: Refrigerate for up to 3 days.)*

INGREDIENTS

8 cups	shredded green cabbage
1¼ tsp	salt
3 cups	grated carrots
Half	red onion, thinly sliced
⅓ cup	vinegar
2 tbsp	vegetable oil
4 tsp	granulated sugar
1 tsp	dry mustard
½ tsp	celery seeds
¼ cup	chopped fresh parsley

Makes 8 servings.
PER SERVING: about 78 cal, 2 g pro, 4 g total fat (trace sat. fat), II g carb, 2 g fibre, 0 mg chol,
328 mg sodium, 306 mg potassium. % RDI: 5% calcium, 5% iron, 39% vit A, 47% vit C, 20% folate.

RAINBOW SLAW

THIS VIVID SLAW STAYS CRUNCHY AND IS CREAMY WITHOUT THE ADDITION
OF MAYONNAISE. IF YOU'RE TOTING THIS SALAD TO A POTLUCK OR PICNIC, PACK THE CHEESE
IN A SEPARATE CONTAINER TO KEEP ALL THE COLOURS AND FLAVOURS BRIGHT.

METHOD

Halve and core apple; julienne (see how-to, page 36). In large bowl, toss apple with lemon juice. Add green and red cabbage, celery and walnuts.

Whisk together sour cream, vinegar, pepper, hot pepper sauce, salt and celery salt; pour over cabbage mixture. Toss to combine. Refrigerate for 2 hours. (*Make-ahead: Cover and refrigerate for up to 24 hours.*) Just before serving, sprinkle with blue cheese.

HOW TO

TOAST WALNUTS

Spread walnuts on rimmed baking sheet; toast in 350°F (180°C) oven until light golden, 6 to 8 minutes. Let cool.

INGREDIENTS

1	red-skinned apple (such as Spartan or Empire) or Granny Smith apple
1½ tsp	lemon juice
2 cups	shredded green cabbage
2 cups	shredded red cabbage
½ cup	sliced celery
¼ cup	chopped toasted walnuts (see how-to, below)
¼ cup	light sour cream
4 tsp	cider vinegar
¼ tsp	pepper
Dash	hot pepper sauce
Pinch	each salt and celery salt
⅓ cup	crumbled blue cheese

Makes 8 servings.
PER SERVING: about 73 cal, 3 g pro, 5 g total fat (2 g sat. fat), 7 g carb, 1 g fibre, 5 mg chol, 96 mg sodium. % RDI: 6% calcium, 3% iron, 2% vit A, 28% vit C, 9% folate.

FENNEL AND PARMESAN COLESLAW

FENNEL IS EXCELLENT IN A SUMMER SALAD BECAUSE IT STAYS CRISP IN DRESSING AND
DOESN'T DISCOLOUR. THE LEMON VINAIGRETTE MELLOWS ITS LICORICE FLAVOUR, SO GIVE THIS
SALAD A TRY EVEN IF FENNEL NORMALLY ISN'T YOUR FAVOURITE.

210

INGREDIENTS

½ tsp	grated lemon zest
3 tbsp	lemon juice
3 tbsp	extra-virgin olive oil
¼ tsp	salt
Pinch	pepper
1	bulb fennel, cored and thinly sliced
2 tsp	coarsely chopped fennel fronds
Half	small red or sweet onion, thinly sliced
½ cup	shaved Parmesan cheese

METHOD

In large bowl, whisk together lemon zest, lemon juice, oil, salt and pepper.

Add fennel, fennel fronds and onion; toss to combine. Cover and refrigerate for 4 hours. *(Make-ahead: Refrigerate for up to 24 hours.)*

Just before serving, add Parmesan cheese; toss to combine.

TEST KITCHEN TIP

For a boost of colour, add up to 2 tbsp more chopped fennel fronds if your fennel bulb has a lot attached.

PHOTO PAGE 147

Makes 6 to 8 servings.

PER EACH OF 8 SERVINGS: about 85 cal, 3 g pro, 7 g total fat (2 g sat. fat), 4 g carb, 1 g fibre, 5 mg chol, 198 mg sodium, 146 mg potassium. % RDI: 9% calcium, 2% iron, 1% vit A, 12% vit C, 5% folate.

COLESLAW
with cider vinaigrette

COLESLAW IS A BARBECUE MUST-HAVE, AND THIS ONE IS SURE TO PLEASE ANY CROWD.
THE LONGER IT SITS, THE MORE FLAVOURFUL IT GETS, SO MAKE IT A DAY IN ADVANCE FOR THE BEST TASTE.

211

METHOD

Cider Vinaigrette: In large bowl, whisk together vinegar, lemon juice, sugar, salt and pepper until sugar is dissolved, about 1 minute. Whisk in oil until blended.

Add cabbage, radishes, onion and parsley; toss to coat. Cover and refrigerate for 2 hours. *(Make-ahead: Refrigerate for up to 24 hours.)*

CHANGE IT UP
TROPICAL COLESLAW

Substitute lime juice for vinegar and fresh cilantro for parsley. Add 1 cup diced peeled cored pineapple and 1 mango, peeled, pitted and diced.

INGREDIENTS

10 cups	shredded green cabbage
1½ cups	thinly sliced radishes
Half	Vidalia or other sweet onion, thinly sliced
2 tbsp	chopped fresh parsley

Cider Vinaigrette:

¼ cup	cider vinegar
1 tbsp	lemon juice
2 tsp	granulated sugar
½ tsp	salt
¼ tsp	pepper
⅓ cup	extra-virgin olive oil

PHOTO
PAGE 194

Makes 10 to 12 servings.

PER EACH OF 12 SERVINGS: about 78 cal, 1 g pro, 6 g total fat (1 g sat. fat), 6 g carb, 1 g fibre, 0 mg chol, 114 mg sodium, 204 mg potassium. % RDI: 3% calcium, 4% iron, 2% vit A, 38% vit C, 15% folate.

MACADAMIA NUT SLAW

MACADAMIA NUTS ARE THE IDEAL CRUNCHY GARNISH FOR THIS BRIGHTLY COLOURED SLAW. ASIAN PEARS ARE DELIGHTFULLY CRISP AND VERY MILD; BOSC PEARS ARE A GOOD, EASY-TO-FIND SUBSTITUTE.

212

INGREDIENTS

Quarter	head each napa cabbage and red cabbage
2	small carrots
2	green onions
1	Asian or Bosc pear, peeled, halved and cored
Half	sweet red pepper
½ cup	chopped macadamia nuts
3 tbsp	chopped fresh mint

Chili Ginger Dressing:

¼ cup	vegetable oil
¼ cup	unseasoned rice vinegar
4 tsp	lime juice
2 tsp	finely grated fresh ginger
½ tsp	sweet Asian chili sauce
¼ tsp	salt

METHOD

Chili Ginger Dressing: Whisk together oil, vinegar, lime juice, ginger, chili sauce and salt; set aside.

Thinly slice napa and red cabbages; place in large bowl. Julienne carrots, green onions, pear and red pepper (see how-to, page 36); add to bowl. Pour dressing over top; toss to coat. (*Make-ahead: Cover and refrigerate for up to 6 hours.*)

Just before serving, sprinkle with macadamia nuts and mint.

TEST KITCHEN TIP

If you don't have any sweet Asian chili sauce, use ½ tsp hot pepper sauce mixed with ¼ tsp granulated sugar.

Makes 8 servings.

PER SERVING: about 156 cal, 2 g pro, 14 g total fat (2 g sat. fat), 10 g carb, 3 g fibre, 0 mg chol, 93 mg sodium. % RDI: 5% calcium, 6% iron, 23% vit A, 70% vit C, 19% folate.

NOTES FROM THE TEST KITCHEN

FRUIT & VEGETABLE

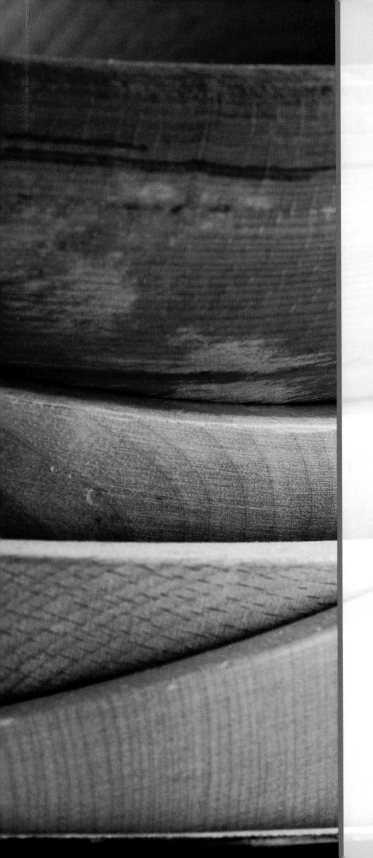

RECIPES

CAULIFLOWER AND SPICED GOUDA SALAD

GOUDA CHEESE IS FAMOUS FOR ITS SPICED VARIETIES, MADE WITH A NUMBER OF DIFFERENT EXOTIC SEASONINGS. THE SPICES ADD AN INTERESTING DEPTH OF FLAVOUR TO THIS ALREADY APPEALING AND HEARTY COMBINATION OF VEGETABLES, FRUIT AND MEAT.

INGREDIENTS

1	head cauliflower (about 900 g)
1½ cups	diced spiced Gouda cheese (such as cumin, coriander or fenugreek)
1	thick (½-inch/1 cm) slice Black Forest ham (about 225 g), diced
1 cup	diced sweet onion
⅓ cup	diced gherkin pickles (see tip, below)
1	apple, cored and diced
¼ cup	mayonnaise
3 tbsp	each finely chopped fresh parsley and chives
3 tbsp	sour cream
4 tsp	cider vinegar
1 tbsp	gherkin brine from jar
1½ tsp	curry powder
½ tsp	granulated sugar
Pinch	each salt and pepper
Dash	hot pepper sauce
1	head Boston lettuce, separated in leaves

METHOD

Remove any leaves from cauliflower. In large pot of boiling salted water, blanch cauliflower until tender-crisp, about 3 minutes. Drain. Transfer to bowl of ice water; let cool. Drain well; cut into florets.

In large bowl, combine cauliflower, Gouda cheese, ham, onion, pickles and apple.

Whisk together mayonnaise, parsley, chives, sour cream, vinegar, gherkin brine, curry powder, sugar, salt, pepper and hot pepper sauce. Add to cauliflower mixture; toss to coat.

Line plates with lettuce leaves; serve salad in lettuce cups.

TEST KITCHEN TIP

Sweet or sour gherkins are delicious in this salad. Which kind you use depends on your preference. Sour gherkins are also called cornichons. Look for both types in the pickle aisle at the supermarket.

Makes 4 to 6 servings.

PER EACH OF 6 SERVINGS: about 290 cal, 18 g pro, 19 g total fat (8 g sat. fat), 14 g carb, 4 g fibre, 63 mg chol, 1,507 mg sodium, 480 mg potassium. % RDI: 26% calcium, 11% iron, 13% vit A, 83% vit C, 38% folate.

HEIRLOOM CARROT SALAD

PAPER-THIN SLICES OF MULTICOLOURED HEIRLOOM CARROTS MAKE A STUNNING SALAD. REGULAR ORANGE CARROTS ARE JUST AS TASTY, SO SUBSTITUTE THEM IF YOU LIKE.

218

INGREDIENTS

450 g	multicoloured heirloom carrots (about 3)
12	sprigs fresh cilantro
¼ cup	toasted unsalted pepitas (see tip, below)
¼ cup	crumbled feta cheese

Orange Cumin Vinaigrette:

¼ tsp	cumin seeds, crushed
2 tbsp	orange juice
1 tbsp	vegetable oil
1 tbsp	lemon juice
½ tsp	ground coriander
½ tsp	liquid honey
Pinch	each salt and pepper

METHOD

Using mandoline or vegetable peeler, slice carrots lengthwise into paper-thin strips. Place carrots and cilantro in bowl of ice water; let stand for 3 minutes. Drain and pat dry.

Orange Cumin Vinaigrette: Meanwhile, in small dry skillet over medium-high heat, toast cumin seeds until darkened and just beginning to pop, about 30 seconds. Transfer to large bowl. Whisk in orange juice, oil, lemon juice, coriander, honey, salt and pepper.

Add carrots, cilantro and pepitas to vinaigrette; toss to coat. Sprinkle with feta cheese.

TEST KITCHEN TIP

Pepitas are hulled green pumpkin seeds and are the richest natural source of magnesium. They are available raw, roasted, unsalted and salted. Look for them in supermarkets, bulk and natural foods stores, and Latin American markets.

Makes 4 servings.

PER SERVING: about 185 cal, 7 g pro, 12 g total fat (3 g sat. fat), 15 g carb, 5 g fibre, 9 mg chol, 190 mg sodium, 542 mg potassium. % RDI: 9% calcium, 20% iron, 196% vit A, 22% vit C, 19% folate.

JICAMA SALAD
with avocado purée

WHO SAYS FALL SIDE DISHES HAVE TO BE FULL OF ROASTED VEGETABLES? THIS CRISP SALAD LOOKS UNCONVENTIONAL, BUT TRUST US—IT'S A CROWD-PLEASER THAT WILL GET GOBBLED UP IN RECORD TIME.

219

METHOD

Toss together pepitas, ½ tsp each of the oil and salt, half of the cayenne pepper and the allspice. Toast on parchment paper–lined rimmed baking sheet in 350°F (180°C) oven until light golden, 6 to 8 minutes. Let cool.

Cut kernels off corn cobs (see how-to, page 203); toss with 1 tbsp of the remaining oil and a pinch of the remaining cayenne pepper. Spread on rimmed baking sheet; roast in 425°F (220°C) oven until tender, about 6 minutes. Let cool.

Using chef's knife and following contour of vegetable, peel, quarter and thinly slice jicama; using mandoline, julienne (see how-to, page 36). In large bowl, combine jicama, pepitas, corn, cilantro and mint. Add lime juice and remaining oil, salt and cayenne pepper; toss to coat.

Avocado Purée: In food processor, purée together avocados, lime juice and salt, scraping down side of bowl often. Spread on platter, making ¼-inch (5 mm) thick layer; top with jicama salad.

INGREDIENTS

½ cup	unsalted pepitas (see tip, opposite)
2 tbsp	olive oil
¾ tsp	salt
¼ tsp	cayenne pepper
¼ tsp	ground allspice
2	cobs corn, husked
1	jicama (about 800 g)
⅓ cup	packed fresh cilantro leaves, coarsely chopped
⅓ cup	packed fresh mint leaves, coarsely chopped
3 tbsp	lime juice

Avocado Purée:

2	ripe avocados, pitted, peeled and cut in chunks
1 tbsp	lime juice
½ tsp	salt

Makes 6 servings.

PER SERVING: about 304 cal, 7 g pro, 20 g total fat (3 g sat. fat), 30 g carb, 13 g fibre, 0 mg chol, 500 mg sodium, 738 mg potassium. % RDI: 4% calcium, 26% iron, 6% vit A, 60% vit C, 46% folate.

THREE-PEA SALAD

THIS GORGEOUS, DELICATE SALAD CONTAINS MANY JEWELS OF THE EARLY SPRINGTIME HARVEST. WATERCRESS IS A TASTY ALTERNATIVE TO HARDER-TO-FIND PEA TENDRILS, EXTENDING THE SEASON FOR THIS RECIPE.

METHOD

In saucepan of boiling salted water, cook shelled peas for 1½ minutes. Add sugar snap peas; cook just until tender, about 1 minute. Drain and transfer to bowl of ice water; let cool. Drain well; set aside.

In bowl, whisk together vinegar, honey, salt and pepper; whisk in oil. *(Make-ahead: Refrigerate peas and dressing in separate airtight containers for up to 24 hours. Bring to room temperature.)*

In large bowl, combine shelled peas, snap peas, radishes, green onions and pea tendrils; toss with dressing to coat. Add feta cheese; toss to coat.

INGREDIENTS

1 cup	shelled fresh peas
450 g	sugar snap peas, trimmed
2 tbsp	white balsamic vinegar or wine vinegar
2 tsp	liquid honey
Pinch	each salt and pepper
¼ cup	extra-virgin olive oil
6	radishes, thinly sliced
3	green onions, thinly sliced
4 cups	trimmed fresh pea tendrils (see tip, below) or watercress
¾ cup	crumbled feta cheese

TEST KITCHEN TIP

In the cool early spring, leafy young tendrils (also called pea shoots) appear on sugar snap pea, snow pea and shelling pea plants. They make beautiful garnishes and are excellent in salads. For a quick side dish, sauté pea tendrils briefly with oil and garlic, or blanch them in boiling salted water then drain and drizzle with sesame or extra-virgin olive oil. Chinese cuisine prizes these springtime garden vegetables highly; you'll often find them in Chinese grocery stores in late winter, spring and fall.

Makes 6 servings.

PER SERVING: about 196 cal, 7 g pro, 13 g total fat (4 g sat. fat), 13 g carb, 4 g fibre, 7 mg chol, 444 mg sodium, 365 mg potassium. % RDI: 15% calcium, 15% iron, 23% vit A, 82% vit C, 23% folate.

SALAD OF WHITE AND GREEN ASPARAGUS
with fiddleheads

WHITE ASPARAGUS GROWS COVERED WITH SOIL AND NEVER RECEIVES THE SUNLIGHT NEEDED TO PRODUCE GREEN CHLOROPHYLL. IT IS WONDERFUL BUT CAN BE TRICKY TO FIND, SO USE ALL GREEN IF IT'S NOT AVAILABLE.

INGREDIENTS

1½ cups	fiddleheads (about 225 g), cleaned (see how-to, below)
225 g	green asparagus
225 g	white asparagus
4 cups	mixed greens
1 cup	fresh raspberries (see tip, page 73)
¼ cup	sliced almonds, toasted (see tip, page 44)

Raspberry Vinaigrette:

⅓ cup	extra-virgin olive oil
2 tbsp	raspberry or red wine vinegar
½ tsp	granulated sugar
½ tsp	salt
½ tsp	Dijon mustard
¼ tsp	pepper

METHOD

Raspberry Vinaigrette: Whisk together oil, vinegar, sugar, salt, mustard and pepper; set aside.

In steamer rack over 1 inch (2.5 cm) boiling water, steam fiddleheads until tender-crisp, about 8 minutes. Using slotted spoon, transfer to bowl of ice water; let cool. Drain well; pat dry.

Meanwhile, snap woody ends off green and white asparagus (see how-to, page 175). Steam stalks until tender-crisp, about 4 minutes. Using tongs, transfer to bowl of ice water; let cool. Drain well; pat dry.

In large bowl, toss mixed greens with half of the vinaigrette. Toss together fiddleheads, green and white asparagus, and remaining dressing. Arrange mixed greens on four plates. Using tongs, arrange fiddleheads and asparagus on top; garnish with raspberries and almonds. Drizzle with any remaining dressing.

HOW TO

CLEAN FIDDLEHEADS

Snap off bright green tops from ferns, leaving 2 inches (5 cm) of stem attached and discarding remaining stems. Rub off dry brown casings. Soak fiddleheads in sink half-full of cold water, changing water several times to remove any grit or casing particles. Drain well.

Makes 4 servings.

PER SERVING: about 249 cal, 6 g pro, 22 g total fat (3 g sat. fat), 12 g carb, 5 g fibre, 0 mg chol, 322 mg sodium. % RDI: 8% calcium, 15% iron, 30% vit A, 45% vit C, 78% folate.

MARINATED VEGETABLE SALAD

THIS COLOURFUL, CHUNKY COMBINATION TASTES BEST WHEN MADE A DAY AHEAD TO ALLOW THE FLAVOURS IN THE DRESSING TO REALLY PENETRATE THE VEGETABLES. THIS IS A TERRIFIC DISH TO MAKE AT HARVESTTIME, WHEN ALL THESE VEGGIES ARE AT THEIR PEAK AND AVAILABLE IN FARMER'S MARKETS.

METHOD

In large saucepan of boiling salted water, cover and cook carrots until tender-crisp, about 4 minutes. Using slotted spoon, transfer to bowl of ice water; let cool completely. Using slotted spoon, transfer to large shallow dish.

Repeat with cauliflower, cooking for about 3 minutes. Repeat with green beans, cooking for about 3 minutes. Repeat with zucchini and red pepper, cooking for about 1 minute each.

In bowl, combine garlic, shallot, lemon juice, mustard, thyme, salt, pepper and sugar; slowly whisk in oil until emulsified. Pour over vegetable mixture; toss to combine. Cover and refrigerate for 4 hours. *(Make-ahead: Refrigerate for up to 2 days.)*

Let stand until at room temperature, about 1 hour.

INGREDIENTS

2 cups	chopped carrots
3 cups	cauliflower florets
2 cups	trimmed green beans
1	zucchini, sliced
1	sweet red pepper, sliced
3	cloves garlic, minced
1	shallot, minced
¼ cup	lemon juice
2 tbsp	Dijon mustard
¾ tsp	dried thyme
¼ tsp	each salt and pepper
Pinch	granulated sugar
⅓ cup	extra-virgin olive oil

Makes 8 servings.
PER SERVING: about 122 cal, 2 g pro, 10 g total fat (1 g sat. fat), 9 g carb, 3 g fibre, 0 mg chol, 445 mg sodium. % RDI: 4% calcium, 6% iron, 60% vit A, 78% vit C, 16% folate.

FIDDLEHEAD, PEA AND ASPARAGUS SALAD
with mint vinaigrette

THIS VIBRANT GREEN SALAD CELEBRATES SPRING WITH EVERY BITE. THE OLD-FASHIONED PAIRING OF PEAS AND MINT GETS A NEW LEASE ON LIFE WITH THE ADDITION OF ASPARAGUS AND FIDDLEHEADS.

INGREDIENTS

1 cup	fresh or frozen peas
12	spears asparagus, trimmed (see how-to, page 175) and cut in 5-inch (12 cm) lengths
3 cups	fiddleheads (about 280 g), cleaned (see how-to, page 222)
¼ cup	crumbled soft goat cheese

Mint Vinaigrette:

3 tbsp	extra-virgin olive oil
2 tbsp	lemon juice
¼ tsp	granulated sugar
Pinch	each salt and pepper
¼ cup	packed fresh mint leaves, chopped

METHOD

In large pot of boiling salted water, blanch peas until tender, 1 to 4 minutes. Using slotted spoon, transfer to bowl of ice water; set aside.

In same pot, blanch asparagus until tender-crisp, about 3 minutes. Using slotted spoon, add to peas. In same pot, blanch fiddleheads for 5 minutes. Drain; add to peas. Let cool.

Drain fiddlehead mixture; pat dry. Halve asparagus crosswise.

Mint Vinaigrette: In large bowl, whisk together oil, lemon juice, sugar, salt and pepper; stir in mint. Add fiddlehead mixture; toss to combine. Sprinkle with goat cheese.

Makes 4 servings.

PER SERVING: about 188 cal, 9 g pro, 13 g total fat (3 g sat. fat), 13 g carb, 4 g fibre, 4 mg chol, 437 mg sodium. % RDI: 7% calcium, 21% iron, 42% vit A, 45% vit C, 44% folate.

Exotic Salad Veggies to Try

Lettuce is, by far, not the only option for salads. As a matter of fact, some of the most interesting and mouthwatering choices are ones you may never have thought of. Here are a few to add to your roster.

CELERIAC

Also known as celery root, celeriac is a large, knobby root with lots of small rootlets twisting around it. A relative of regular celery, with a vibrant celery flavour, it's tasty both cooked (in soups and stews) and raw (sliced in salads). Once peeled and trimmed, a large celeriac is reduced to about two-thirds of its original size. Raw slices oxidize quickly, but tossing them with lemon juice or soaking them in acidulated water will slow down the process.

CHAYOTE

A type of summer squash, chayotes look like large, wrinkled, pale green pears. Their delicately flavoured flesh can be thinly sliced and eaten raw, but light cooking further softens the taste. Chayotes are usually prepared like other summer squash for use in salads and can be peeled if desired.

DAIKON RADISH

This large, long, white root is commonly used in Japanese and Korean cooking, as well as in Chinese cuisine, where it is known by the name lo bok. The flesh is tender-crisp and a bit watery, with a strong smell similar to that of cabbage or turnip (which intensifies when the cut radish is stored in the fridge). The flavour is very mild, however; daikon goes well with simple vinaigrettes and is great for making quick pickles.

JICAMA

A large, round, pale beige tuber, with crunchy white flesh, this root vegetable is popular in Mexican cuisine for its refreshingly crisp texture, very mild flavour and slightly starchy feel. It's excellent julienned and simply dressed in salads.

KOHLRABI

Small pale-green heads, with multiple stalks attached to long greens, have a delicate taste that's reminiscent of the tender inside of a broccoli stalk. Actually a type of cabbage, kohlrabi is an attention grabber but is often passed up because it looks a little like an alien's head in the produce section. Once trimmed and peeled, though, the crisp root is wonderful sliced or shredded raw for salads, or sliced and cooked as a side dish.

RUTABAGA

Also known as swede and, confusingly, turnip (which it definitely is not), this large root has waxy skin covering golden flesh. In Canada, it's often served cooked and mashed like potatoes, but raw slices are incredibly tasty in salads, too.

CHAYOTE SALAD

BOTH THE CHAYOTE AND THE DRESSING FOR THIS SALAD CAN BE PREPARED AHEAD. THEN ALL THEY REQUIRE IS A QUICK TOSS AT THE LAST MINUTE BEFORE SERVING. DON'T BE TEMPTED TO DRESS THE SALAD EARLIER—THE LIQUID WILL LEECH OUT OF THE VEGETABLES.

227

METHOD

In saucepan of boiling salted water, boil chayotes until tender-crisp, about 5 minutes. Using tongs, transfer to bowl of ice water; let cool. Drain well. Slice thinly; pat dry with paper towels.

In large bowl, whisk together oil, lime juice, garlic, salt and pepper. Add chayote and cilantro; toss to coat.

INGREDIENTS

3	small chayotes
3 tbsp	extra-virgin olive oil
2 tbsp	lime juice
Half	small clove garlic, finely grated
¼ tsp	each salt and pepper
2 tbsp	chopped fresh cilantro

CHANGE IT UP
ZUCCHINI SALAD

Substitute 3 small zucchini (450 g) for chayotes; simmer, whole, until tender-crisp, about 7 minutes. Trim off ends; continue with recipe.

Makes 6 servings.

PER SERVING: about 80 cal, 1 g pro, 7 g total fat (1 g sat. fat), 4 g carb, 2 g fibre, 0 mg chol, 276 mg sodium, 139 mg potassium. % RDI: 1% calcium, 2% iron, 1% vit A, 12% vit C, 6% folate.

CARROT AND PEANUT SALAD

CARROTS DON'T USUALLY GET TO BE STARS, BUT THIS SALAD MAKES THEM THE MAIN ATTRACTION.
IF YOU'RE PLANNING TO TAKE IT TO A PARTY, CHECK WITH THE HOST ABOUT OTHER GUESTS' FOOD ALLERGIES—
THE PEANUTS (AND EASY-TO-MISS PEANUT OIL) COULD BE DANGEROUS FOR SOME.

228

INGREDIENTS

¼ cup	peanut or vegetable oil
3 tbsp	lime juice
2 tbsp	fish sauce
1 tbsp	granulated sugar
1 tbsp	unseasoned rice vinegar
1 to 3	Thai bird's-eye peppers (or 1 jalapeño pepper), seeded and minced
1	clove garlic, minced
½ tsp	salt
6 cups	shredded carrots
1¼ cups	thinly sliced radishes
¾ cup	unsalted roasted peanuts, coarsely chopped
⅓ cup	chopped fresh cilantro

METHOD

In large bowl, whisk together oil, lime juice, fish sauce, sugar, vinegar, Thai pepper(s), garlic and salt.

Add carrots, radishes, peanuts and cilantro; toss to coat. Let stand for 10 minutes; wearing rubber gloves, tilt bowl and gently press salad to squeeze out excess liquid. Serve immediately or cover and refrigerate for up to 2 hours.

TEST KITCHEN TIP

It's best to dress this salad as close to serving time as possible. Red-skinned radishes are notorious for bleeding their colour onto other ingredients. If you add the dressing too early, the salad will have a distinct pink tinge.

Makes 8 to 10 servings.
PER EACH OF 10 SERVINGS: about 144 cal, 4 g pro, 11 g total fat (2 g sat. fat), 11 g carb, 3 g fibre, 0 mg chol, 440 mg sodium, 333 mg potassium. % RDI: 3% calcium, 3% iron, 80% vit A, 14% vit C, 14% folate.

SPICY CUCUMBER SALAD

LIKE A QUICK-TO-MAKE FIERY PICKLE, THIS SALAD IS REFRESHING ON A HOT DAY WITH GRILLED DISHES.
IF IT'S SUMMERTIME AND YOU CAN GET FIELD CUCUMBERS, CHOOSE SLIMMER, LESS MATURE ONES
FOR A TEXTURE SIMILAR TO THAT OF TENDER HOTHOUSE ENGLISH CUCUMBERS.

230

INGREDIENTS

3	English cucumbers
½ tsp	salt
2 tbsp	lime juice
1 tsp	minced seeded red finger hot pepper
½ tsp	granulated sugar
Pinch	pepper
¼ cup	chopped fresh cilantro

METHOD

Halve cucumbers lengthwise; using spoon, scrape out seeds. Cut each half crosswise into ¼-inch (5 mm) thick slices. Place in colander set over bowl; sprinkle with salt. Let stand for 30 minutes. Drain and gently squeeze out liquid.

In bowl, toss together cucumbers, lime juice, hot pepper, sugar and pepper; cover and refrigerate for 1 hour. (*Make-ahead: Refrigerate for up to 24 hours.*)

Just before serving, stir in cilantro.

Cucumbers naturally contain a lot of liquid, and slices added directly to salads can water them down. When you're using a large number of cucumbers as a main ingredient, as in this salad, salt them first and drain off the resulting liquid to ensure a tasty, full-flavoured result.

Makes 8 servings.

PER SERVING: about 12 cal, 1 g pro, trace total fat (0 g sat. fat), 2 g carb, 1 g fibre, 0 mg chol, 73 mg sodium. % RDI: 1% calcium, 1% iron, 1% vit A, 8% vit C, 5% folate.

ORANGE AND BEET SALAD
with parmesan curls

PAPER-THIN CURLS OF PARMIGIANO-REGGIANO ACCENTUATE THIS SALAD'S NUTTY NOTES. PARMESAN OR GRANA PADANO CHEESE ARE BUDGET-FRIENDLY SUBSTITUTES, BUT THE REAL STUFF IS WORTH THE SPLURGE.

METHOD

Walnut Shallot Vinaigrette: Whisk together oil, shallot, vinegar, honey, salt and pepper; set aside. *(Make-ahead: Cover and refrigerate for up to 2 days.)*

Trim off beet tops, leaving 1 inch (2.5 cm) of stems attached; leave roots attached. In saucepan of boiling salted water, cover and cook beets until fork-tender, 25 to 30 minutes. Drain; let cool. Peel beets; cut crosswise into ¼-inch (5 mm) thick slices.

Cut off rind and outer membrane of oranges. Cut crosswise into ¼-inch (5 mm) thick slices. *(Make-ahead: Place beets and oranges in separate bowls; cover and refrigerate for up to 24 hours.)*

In small dry skillet, toast walnuts over medium-low heat, stirring often, until lightly browned, about 3 minutes. Let cool.

Using vegetable peeler, shave Parmigiano-Reggiano cheese into thin curls.

Mound arugula on platter or individual plates. Overlap beets and oranges in centre. Sprinkle with walnuts; drizzle with vinaigrette. Scatter cheese over top.

INGREDIENTS

4	beets (about 450 g)
3	navel oranges
⅓ cup	walnut pieces
1	piece (60 g) Parmigiano-Reggiano or Parmesan cheese
2 cups	arugula or watercress, trimmed

Walnut Shallot Vinaigrette:

¼ cup	walnut or extra-virgin olive oil
2 tbsp	minced shallot or onion
2 tbsp	wine vinegar
1 tsp	liquid honey
Pinch	each salt and pepper

PHOTO
PAGE 232

Makes 4 servings.

PER SERVING: about 348 cal, 10 g pro, 24 g total fat (4 g sat. fat), 27 g carb, 6 g fibre, 12 mg chol, 494 mg sodium. % RDI: 24% calcium, 12% iron, 11% vit A, 113% vit C, 65% folate.

**ORANGE AND
BEET SALAD**

with parmesan curls

PAGE 231

SUMMER VEGETABLE SALAD
with sherry vinegar dressing

A RAINBOW OF VEGGIES MAKES THIS DISH A MUST FOR BARBECUES AND PICNICS. JAPANESE OR OTHER ASIAN EGGPLANTS ARE SLIMMER AND MORE DELICATELY FLAVOURED THAN BABY ITALIAN EGGPLANTS, BUT EITHER WILL WORK.

234

INGREDIENTS

1	Japanese eggplant (about 150 g)
1	zucchini
3 tbsp	extra-virgin olive oil
¼ tsp	each salt and pepper
1	sweet yellow or orange pepper
1	small red onion
Half	head radicchio (180 g head)
¼ cup	shredded fresh basil (see how-to, page 254)
¼ cup	shaved Parmesan cheese

Sherry Vinegar Dressing:

2 tbsp	extra-virgin olive oil
1 tbsp	sherry vinegar
1	small clove garlic, minced
½ tsp	Dijon mustard
Pinch	granulated sugar

METHOD

Sherry Vinegar Dressing: Whisk together oil, vinegar, garlic, mustard and sugar; set aside. (*Make-ahead: Cover and refrigerate for up to 24 hours.*)

Cut eggplant and zucchini into generous ¼-inch (5 mm) thick slices; place in bowl. Toss with 4 tsp of the oil and a pinch each of the salt and pepper.

Cut yellow pepper into quarters; seed. Cut onion into ¼-inch (5 mm) thick slices. Brush with 4 tsp of the remaining oil and pinch each of the remaining salt and pepper.

Place vegetables on greased grill over medium-high heat; close lid and grill, turning once, until browned and tender, 10 to 15 minutes. Cut peppers into strips. Separate onions into rings.

Meanwhile, leaving core intact, cut radicchio into four wedges. Brush with remaining oil; sprinkle with remaining salt and pepper. Add to grill; close lid and grill, turning once, until core is tender when pierced with fork and leaves are mostly browned, about 4 minutes. Cut out core.

On platter or in bowl, toss together grilled vegetables, dressing and basil. Garnish with Parmesan cheese.

Makes 4 to 6 servings.

PER EACH OF 6 SERVINGS: about 155 cal, 3 g pro, 13 g total fat (2 g sat. fat), 9 g carb, 2 g fibre, 4 mg chol, 171 mg sodium. % RDI: 6% calcium, 4% iron, 5% vit A, 53% vit C, 11% folate.

CAPRESE SALAD

CELEBRATE THE SUMMER'S RIPEST TOMATOES AND BASIL WITH THIS TASTY, CLASSIC ITALIAN RECIPE. THOUGH NAMED FOR THE ISLAND OF CAPRI, THE SALAD IS ACTUALLY FOUND ALL OVER ITALY AND THE REST OF THE WORLD.

METHOD

In food processor or blender, purée ⅓ cup of the basil, oil, vinegar, salt and pepper until smooth. *(Make-ahead: Refrigerate in airtight container for up to 4 hours; shake before using.)*

Cut mozzarella into ¼-inch (5 mm) thick slices. Cut tomatoes into ½-inch (1 cm) thick slices.

On large serving platter, alternately layer cheese, tomatoes and remaining basil in concentric circles. Sprinkle with onion. *(Make-ahead: Cover and refrigerate for up to 4 hours.)*

Just before serving, drizzle dressing over salad.

INGREDIENTS

1⅓ cups	lightly packed fresh basil leaves
¼ cup	extra-virgin olive oil
4 tsp	balsamic vinegar
Pinch	each salt and pepper
1	ball (250 g) fresh mozzarella cheese (see tip, below)
4	tomatoes, preferably plum
¼ cup	thinly sliced red onion

There are two categories of mozzarella. Fresh mozzarella is another name for the high-moisture variety; it's moist, snowy white and very soft. Fresh mozzarella is ideal uncooked in salads like this Caprese. It's also luscious on traditional Italian-style pizza, but it softens more than it melts. Low-moisture mozzarella is the typical choice for pizza in North America: The drier, yellowish balls shred nicely and melt to the stringy, gooey texture that people expect.

Makes 8 servings.

PER SERVING: about 144 cal, 6 g pro, 13 g total fat (5 g sat. fat), 2 g carb, 1 g fibre, 16 mg chol, 39 mg sodium, 113 mg potassium. % RDI: 10% calcium, 3% iron, 13% vit A, 8% vit C, 5% folate.

HEIRLOOM TOMATOES
with basil

PERUSE LOCAL MARKETS FOR A SELECTION OF TOMATOES IN DIFFERENT SIZES, SHAPES AND COLOURS.
IF YOU CAN'T FIND HEIRLOOMS, DON'T WORRY—THIS SALAD IS SCRUMPTIOUS WITH ANY TOMATO VARIETY.

METHOD

Cut tomatoes into ½-inch (1 cm) thick slices; arrange in centre of serving platter.

Sprinkle with salt and pepper; drizzle with oil and vinegar. Sprinkle with basil.

INGREDIENTS

900 g	mixed heirloom tomatoes
Pinch	each salt and pepper
1 tbsp	extra-virgin olive oil
1 tbsp	wine vinegar
4	leaves fresh basil, shredded (see how-to, page 254)

TEST KITCHEN TIP

An heirloom tomato salad like this practically begs to be served with cheese. While you're at the farmer's market checking out all the varieties of tomatoes, keep your eyes peeled for locally made feta or other dry, salty cheeses. Crusty bread is another must-have alongside this salad. The oil, vinegar and tomato juices are so luscious, you need to sop up every last drop. Look for rustic French-style boules, baguettes, ciabatta or other artisanal breads. Try one studded with salty black olives for a taste sensation.

Makes 6 to 8 servings.
PER EACH OF 8 SERVINGS: about 35 cal, 1 g pro, 2 g total fat (trace sat. fat), 4 g carb, 1 g fibre, 0 mg chol, 6 mg sodium. % RDI: 1% calcium, 2% iron, 9% vit A, 23% vit C, 8% folate.

CUCUMBER HERB SALAD

INEXPENSIVE FIELD CUCUMBERS ARE JUST THE THING FOR THIS LIGHT AND
FRESH SALAD. IF IT'S NOT SUMMER, WHEN FIELD CUKES ARE IN SEASON,
YOU CAN USE A SIMILAR WEIGHT OF ENGLISH CUCUMBERS.

238

INGREDIENTS

4	cucumbers (about 1.35 kg)
½ cup	fresh cilantro leaves
4	green onions, sliced
2 tbsp	chopped fresh mint

Dressing:

3 tbsp	extra-virgin olive oil
2 tbsp	lemon juice
1 tbsp	white wine vinegar
1	shallot, minced
1	clove garlic, minced
¼ tsp	each salt and pepper

METHOD

Peel and quarter cucumbers lengthwise; using spoon, scrape out seeds. Chop cucumbers and place in large bowl. Coarsely chop cilantro; add to cucumbers along with green onions and mint.

Dressing: Whisk together oil, lemon juice, vinegar, shallot, garlic, salt and pepper. Pour over cucumber mixture; toss to coat. Refrigerate for 2 hours. *(Make-ahead: Cover and refrigerate for up to 24 hours.)*

Mint is a herb you can grow without trying at all. Actually, it's so easy to grow that you really have to watch it—when planted directly in the garden, mint tends to go wild and elbow out other plants. But a pot of mint just outside the kitchen door is great for cooking in the summer. Chop it and add to salads, make mint jelly to go with roast lamb, or maybe even dry a bunch of it to make tea when the weather turns cold. Spearmint, or English mint, is the type we use when we call for just "mint," but you can experiment with more exotic varieties. Fresh peppermint is excellent, too, but save it for making desserts, teas and sweets, rather than salads.

Makes 8 servings.

PER SERVING: about 60 cal, 1 g pro, 5 g total fat (1 g sat. fat), 3 g carb, 1 g fibre, 0 mg chol, 76 mg sodium. % RDI: 2% calcium, 4% iron, 2% vit A, 8% vit C, 8% folate.

WALDORF SALAD

ORIGINALLY THE BRAINCHILD OF A CHEF AT THE WALDORF HOTEL IN NEW YORK, THIS FRUIT, NUT AND VEGETABLE SALAD IS A CLASSIC. THE WHIPPED CREAM MAY SOUND UNCONVENTIONAL, BUT IT MAKES THE RICH-TASTING DRESSING FEEL LIGHT AS A FEATHER.

METHOD

Spread walnut halves on rimmed baking sheet; toast in 350°F (180°C) oven until golden and fragrant, 6 to 8 minutes. Let cool. Coarsely chop; set aside.

In large bowl, whip cream until soft peaks form; fold in mayonnaise, lemon juice, salt and pepper.

Fold in walnuts, celery and apples. Refrigerate for 1 hour.

INGREDIENTS

1 cup	walnut halves
¼ cup	whipping cream (35%)
3 tbsp	mayonnaise
1 tbsp	lemon juice
¼ tsp	each salt and pepper
1 cup	sliced celery
2	apples (Idared and/or Red Delicious), cored and sliced

You might be tempted to use light mayonnaise rather than full-fat in your Waldorf Salad—but resist. There isn't much in this recipe (plus, you're adding cream, anyway!), and the full-fat version makes the dressing creamy and rich. Light mayonnaise would give it a sweet-tart edge and detract from the other flavours.

Makes 6 to 8 servings.

PER EACH OF 8 SERVINGS: about 180 cal, 3 g pro, 16 g total fat (3 g sat. fat), 8 g carb, 2 g fibre, 12 mg chol, 116 mg sodium, 154 mg potassium. % RDI: 3% calcium, 4% iron, 4% vit A, 5% vit C, 10% folate.

GREEN BEAN, MUSHROOM AND FENNEL SALAD

A GORGEOUS SALAD IS ALWAYS WELCOME AT AN ELEGANT DINNER PARTY,
AND THIS ONE DOESN'T DISAPPOINT: SHREDS OF LICORICE-SCENTED FENNEL MINGLE WITH
TENDER-CRISP BEANS AND MARINATED MUSHROOMS. WHAT MORE COULD YOU ASK FOR?

241

METHOD

In large bowl, whisk together oil, lemon juice, dill, garlic, salt and pepper. Add mushrooms and toss to coat. Let stand for 15 minutes, stirring occasionally.

Meanwhile, halve green beans diagonally. In saucepan of boiling water, blanch green beans until tender-crisp, 3 to 5 minutes. Using slotted spoon, transfer to bowl of ice water; let cool. Drain well; pat dry with towel.

Add beans and fennel to mushroom mixture; toss to coat. *(Make-ahead: Cover and refrigerate for up to 4 hours.)*

INGREDIENTS

⅓ cup	extra-virgin olive oil
¼ cup	lemon juice
3 tbsp	chopped fresh dill
1	clove garlic, minced
¾ tsp	salt
¼ tsp	pepper
450 g	small cremini mushrooms, quartered
450 g	green beans
Half	bulb fennel, cored and thinly sliced

Makes 12 servings.

PER SERVING: about 76 cal, 2 g pro, 6 g total fat (1 g sat. fat), 5 g carb, 2 g fibre, 0 mg chol, 152 mg sodium, 262 mg potassium. % RDI: 2% calcium, 4% iron, 2% vit A, 10% vit C, 9% folate.

GRILLED EGGPLANT SALAD

THIS DISH IS A BIT MORE LIKE A FRESH RELISH THAN A SALAD, BUT IT MAKES A GOOD
ADDITION TO A PICNIC OR BARBECUE MENU. IT MAKES A WONDERFUL
SIDE WITH GRILLED MEATS, ESPECIALLY LAMB.

INGREDIENTS

2	eggplants (900 g total)
4	green onions, thinly sliced
¼ cup	chopped fresh parsley
¼ cup	chopped fresh cilantro
2	cloves garlic, minced
¼ cup	extra-virgin olive oil
2 tbsp	lemon juice
¾ tsp	salt
¼ tsp	pepper
3 tbsp	chopped walnuts (optional), toasted (see tip, page 209)

METHOD

Prick eggplants all over. Place on greased grill over medium-low heat or on rimmed baking sheet; close lid and grill or bake in 350°F (180°C) oven, turning often on grill, until softened and charred, about 50 minutes. Let cool on plate.

Peel and discard skin and any juices from eggplants; coarsely chop flesh and transfer to serving bowl.

Stir in green onions, parsley, cilantro, garlic, oil, lemon juice, salt and pepper. Cover and refrigerate for 1 hour. (*Make-ahead: Refrigerate for up to 8 hours.*)

Just before serving, sprinkle with walnuts (if using).

Makes 8 servings.

PER SERVING: about 98 cal, 2 g pro, 7 g total fat (2 g sat. fat), 7 g carb, 2 g fibre, 0 mg chol, 217 mg sodium, 161 mg potassium. % RDI: 7% iron, 14% vit C, 7% folate.

NECTARINE AND TOMATO SALAD

TOMATOES AND NECTARINES MIGHT SEEM LIKE AN UNUSUAL
COMBINATION, BUT THEY'RE IN SEASON AT THE SAME TIME AND THEIR FLAVOURS GO
TOGETHER BEAUTIFULLY. THIS SALAD IS AS PRETTY AS IT IS TASTY.

243

METHOD

Cut nectarines in half and remove pits; cut each half into six wedges. Halve and core yellow and red tomatoes; cut each half into four wedges. Arrange nectarines and tomatoes on platter.

Easy Lemon Dressing: Whisk together oil, lemon zest and lemon juice. Drizzle over salad. Sprinkle with feta cheese, basil, salt and pepper.

INGREDIENTS

4	nectarines
2	yellow tomatoes
2	red tomatoes
⅓ cup	crumbled light feta cheese
8	fresh basil leaves, coarsely torn or chopped
½ tsp	coarse sea salt or coarse salt
¼ tsp	pepper

Easy Lemon Dressing:

¼ cup	extra-virgin olive oil
2 tsp	grated lemon zest
2 tbsp	lemon juice

Makes 4 servings.

PER SERVING: about 238 cal, 6 g pro, 17 g total fat (3 g sat. fat), 21 g carb, 3 g fibre, 6 mg chol, 346 mg sodium, 710 mg potassium. % RDI: 6% calcium, 9% iron, 13% vit A, 50% vit C, 23% folate.

RAINBOW VEGGIE SALAD

SIMPLY DRESSED WITH OIL, VINEGAR AND HONEY, THIS CRUNCHY VEGGIE-PACKED
SALAD IS EASY TO ASSEMBLE AND MAKES THE BEST BROWN BAG LUNCH. SHREDDING
THE VEGETABLES ENSURES YOU GET A LITTLE BIT OF EVERYTHING IN EACH BITE.

244

INGREDIENTS

2 tbsp	olive oil
2 tbsp	vinegar or cider vinegar
1 tsp	liquid honey
¼ tsp	each salt and pepper
2 cups	thinly sliced red cabbage
1 cup	shredded carrot
1 cup	shredded zucchini
1 cup	bite-size broccoli florets
¼ cup	unsalted roasted sunflower seeds

METHOD

In bowl, stir together oil, vinegar, honey, salt and pepper
until blended.

Add cabbage, carrot, zucchini, broccoli and sunflower
seeds; toss to coat. Let stand for 20 minutes before serving.
(Make-ahead: Cover and refrigerate for up to 2 days.)

TEST KITCHEN TIP

This salad takes a lot of shredding. It's a good candidate for using a
mandoline or the shredder blade on your food processor. Either will
shred all the cabbage, zucchini and carrot quickly, saving you time.

Makes 4 servings.
PER SERVING: about 143 cal, 3 g pro, 11 g total fat (1 g sat. fat), 11 g carb, 3 g fibre, 0 mg chol,
32 mg sodium, 378 mg potassium. % RDI: 4% calcium, 6% iron, 39% vit A, 73% vit C, 25% folate.

SQUASH AND GOAT CHEESE SALAD

THIS DISH MAKES A LOVELY STARTER FOR AN AUTUMN LUNCHEON OR DINNER PARTY. IT'S ALSO ULTRACONVENIENT, BECAUSE THE SQUASH IS SCRUMPTIOUS EITHER WARM OR COLD. PANKO BREAD CRUMBS ARE COARSER AND CRISPIER THAN REGULAR ONES; LOOK FOR THEM IN THE JAPANESE SECTION OF GROCERY STORES AND IN ASIAN MARKETS.

METHOD

Cut each squash in half; using spoon, scrape out seeds. Remove stems; cut each squash crosswise into six half-moon slices about ½ inch (1 cm) thick. Place in large bowl; set aside.

Whisk together olive oil, vinegar, vegetable oil, mustard, garlic, salt, pepper, thyme and sugar. Add 3 tbsp of the oil mixture to squash, tossing to coat; place on foil-lined rimmed baking sheet. Roast in 375°F (190°C) oven, turning halfway through, until tender and golden, about 30 minutes.

Crispy Goat Cheese: Meanwhile, cut goat cheese into 12 slices; flatten slightly to make about 2½-inch (6 cm) rounds. In small bowl, whisk egg with 1 tsp water. In separate small bowl, toss together panko, parsley, salt and pepper. Dip cheese into egg, then panko mixture, pressing to coat. Place on parchment paper–lined rimmed baking sheet. *(Make-ahead: Cover and refrigerate squash and cheese separately for up to 6 hours.)*

In nonstick skillet, heat about 2 tbsp oil over medium heat; fry goat cheese, in batches, turning once and adding more oil if necessary, until crisp and golden, about 3 minutes. Drain on paper towel–lined plate.

In bowl, toss greens with remaining oil mixture; divide among six plates. Arrange four slices of the squash and two slices of the goat cheese around each salad.

INGREDIENTS

2	small squash (such as acorn or buttercup), each about 750 g
¼ cup	extra-virgin olive oil
3 tbsp	white balsamic vinegar or white wine vinegar
2 tbsp	vegetable oil
1 tsp	Dijon mustard
1	clove garlic, minced
¼ tsp	each salt and pepper
¼ tsp	dried thyme
Pinch	granulated sugar
8 cups	mixed greens

Crispy Goat Cheese:

1	log (300 g) soft goat cheese
1	egg
½ cup	panko or dried bread crumbs
¼ cup	minced fresh parsley
¼ tsp	each salt and pepper
2 tbsp	vegetable oil (approx)

Makes 6 servings.

PER SERVING: about 435 cal, 14 g pro, 30 g total fat (10 g sat. fat), 30 g carb, 4 g fibre, 54 mg chol, 487 mg sodium. % RDI: 18% calcium, 25% iron, 39% vit A, 45% vit C, 49% folate.

SHREDDED BRUSSELS SPROUT SALAD

YOU MAY NOT NORMALLY LIKE COOKED BRUSSELS SPROUTS, BUT DON'T PASS THIS SALAD UP.
WHEN THE SPROUTS ARE SHREDDED RAW, THEY TASTE LIKE THE TINY CABBAGES THEY ARE.
AND WITH CRISP PROSCIUTTO ON TOP? HEAVEN!

METHOD

In large bowl, whisk together mayonnaise, Parmesan cheese, lemon juice, mustard, anchovy paste, garlic, Worcestershire sauce and pepper. Add brussels sprouts; toss to coat. Set aside.

In skillet, heat oil over medium heat; cook prosciutto until crisp. Add prosciutto with oil to sprouts mixture; toss to coat. Let stand until slightly wilted, about 10 minutes.

INGREDIENTS

3 tbsp	light mayonnaise
2 tbsp	grated Parmesan cheese
1 tbsp	lemon juice
1 tsp	Dijon mustard
1 tsp	anchovy paste (see tip, page 37)
1	large clove garlic, minced
½ tsp	Worcestershire sauce
Pinch	pepper
4 cups	shredded brussels sprouts (about 16 sprouts), see tip, below
2 tbsp	extra-virgin olive oil
2 tbsp	diced prosciutto or bacon

TEST KITCHEN TIP

Brussels sprouts are too small to shred with a mandoline without shredding your fingers. Thinly slicing them with a chef's knife is your best (and safest) bet.

Makes 4 servings.

PER SERVING: about 160 cal, 5 g pro, 12 g total fat (2 g sat. fat), 10 g carb, 3 g fibre, 10 mg chol, 262 mg sodium. % RDI: 7% calcium, 11% iron, 9% vit A, 127% vit C, 25% folate.

TROPICAL FRUIT SALAD

THIS EXOTIC FRUIT SALAD IS A BIT OF AN INDULGENCE FOR
FRIENDS AND FAMILY, BUT IT'S SO WORTH THE WORK. SAVE THE LEFTOVER FRUIT AND ANY
EXTRA FRUIT SALAD, AND BLEND THEM INTO A SMOOTHIE THE NEXT DAY.

INGREDIENTS

Half	pineapple
1	papaya
Half	pomegranate
3	Minneolas, tangerines or clementines
2	kiwifruit
2 tbsp	lime juice
1 tbsp	liquid honey
½ tsp	grated fresh ginger
1	star fruit, sliced

METHOD

Peel, core and cut pineapple into bite-size chunks. Peel, halve, seed and cut papaya into bite-size chunks. Remove seeds from pomegranate (see how-to, page 39). Peel, halve and section two of the Minneolas. Peel and cut kiwifruit into bite-size chunks. Place fruit in large bowl.

Cut remaining Minneola in half lengthwise. Juice one half; set juice aside. Peel and section remaining half; add to bowl.

In separate bowl, whisk together reserved Minneola juice, lime juice, honey and ginger; pour over fruit. Toss to coat. Cover and refrigerate for 1 hour. *(Make-ahead: Refrigerate for up to 24 hours.)*

Just before serving, garnish with star fruit.

Makes 6 to 8 servings.

PER EACH OF 8 SERVINGS: about 74 cal, I g pro, trace total fat (0 g sat. fat), I9 g carb, 2 g fibre, 0 mg chol, 3 mg sodium, 293 mg potassium. % RDI: 3% calcium, 2% iron, 9% vit A, II7% vit C, 9% folate.

GRILLED FRUIT
with honeyed crème fraîche

THE BUTTER, BOURBON AND HONEY GLAZE FOR THIS FANCY FRUIT SALAD ADDS FLAVOUR AND
HELPS CARAMELIZE THE LUSCIOUS PEACHES, MANGOES AND PINEAPPLE ON THE GRILL. CRÈME FRAÎCHE IS A
DECADENT TOPPING, BUT GREEK YOGURT OR SOUR CREAM ARE ALSO GOOD CHOICES.

METHOD

Honeyed Crème Fraîche: Stir together crème fraîche, honey and vanilla. *(Make-ahead: Cover and refrigerate for up to 24 hours.)*

Stir together butter, bourbon and honey. Place peaches, pineapple and mango on greased grill over medium heat; close lid and grill, brushing with butter mixture and turning frequently, until softened and caramelized, about 5 minutes.

Arrange pineapple rings on four dessert plates; top with peaches and mango. Spoon crème fraîche mixture over top; sprinkle with mint.

INGREDIENTS

2 tbsp	butter, melted
1 tbsp	bourbon
1 tbsp	liquid honey
4	small peaches, halved and pitted
4	rings fresh pineapple (½ inch/ 1 cm thick)
1	large mango, peeled, pitted and cut in large wedges
2 tbsp	chopped fresh mint

Honeyed Crème Fraîche:

¼ cup	crème fraîche
2 tsp	liquid honey
½ tsp	vanilla

For best results, use fruit that is ripe but still firm so it holds its shape on the grill. Anything too ripe may fall apart and slip through the grates.

Makes 4 servings.

PER SERVING: about 257 cal, 2 g pro, 12 g total fat (8 g sat. fat), 37 g carb, 4 g fibre, 40 mg chol, 49 mg sodium, 367 mg potassium. % RDI: 3% calcium, 6% iron, 22% vit A, 63% vit C, 7% folate.

GRAPEFRUIT AND FENNEL SALAD

FOR ADDED FLAIR, SPRINKLE THIS REFRESHING CITRUS SALAD WITH FLAKY SEA SALT
AND TOASTED PECAN HALVES. ADD THIS DISH TO A HOLIDAY MENU DURING THE WINTER, WHEN
GRAPEFRUITS ARE IN SEASON, FOR A TASTE OF SUNSHINE.

METHOD

Peel grapefruit. Working over bowl, cut off outer membrane. Cut between membrane and pulp to release sections into bowl. Squeeze membranes to extract remaining juice. Remove 2 tbsp of the juice; set aside for dressing. Strain sections and set aside, saving any remaining juice for another purpose.

White Balsamic and Mustard Dressing: In large bowl, whisk together reserved grapefruit juice, vinegar, mustard, salt and pepper; slowly whisk in oil until emulsified.

Add lettuce, arugula, watercress and fennel; toss to coat. Garnish with reserved grapefruit sections.

INGREDIENTS

1	ruby red grapefruit
4 cups	torn Bibb lettuce
2 cups	trimmed arugula, torn
2 cups	trimmed watercress
½ cup	thinly sliced cored fennel bulb

White Balsamic and Mustard Dressing:

4 tsp	white balsamic vinegar
½ tsp	grainy mustard
¼ tsp	each salt and pepper
3 tbsp	canola or vegetable oil

Makes 6 to 8 servings.

PER EACH OF 8 SERVINGS: about 67 cal, I g pro, 5 g total fat (trace sat. fat), 4 g carb, I g fibre,
0 mg chol, 88 mg sodium, 220 mg potassium. % RDI: 4% calcium, 3% iron, II% vit A, 33% vit C,
18% folate.

MINTY MELON AND BLACKBERRIES

THIS ELEGANT FRUIT SALAD GETS A PALATE-PLEASING
LIFT FROM FRESH MINT. AS WELL AS BEING A CALORIE-WISE DESSERT
(WITHOUT ADDED SUGAR), IT'S ALSO BRIMMING WITH VITAMIN C.

254

INGREDIENTS

Half	honeydew melon
1	ruby red grapefruit
1 tbsp	granulated sugar
1 tbsp	lime juice
½ cup	fresh blackberries (see tip, page 73)
2 tsp	shredded fresh mint leaves (see how-to, below)

METHOD

Scrape seeds from melon. Cut into eight wedges; cut off rind. Set aside.

Working over bowl, cut off outer rind and membrane of grapefruit. Cut between membrane and pulp to release sections into bowl. Squeeze membranes to extract remaining juice. Whisk sugar and lime juice into bowl; stir in blackberries and half of the mint.

Arrange melon and grapefruit sections on plates; spoon blackberry mixture over top. Sprinkle with remaining mint.

HOW TO

SHRED, OR CHIFFONADE, FRESH HERBS

Chiffonade is the technical term for rolling up and cutting leaves into fine shreds, such as the mint leaves in this fruit salad. Literally translated, this French word means "made of rags." It's easier to do with larger mint leaves, so use ones closer to the root. Wash the mint sprigs and gently pat dry. Pull the leaves off the stem and stack them about a half-dozen high. Then roll them up tightly from top to bottom, with the thick central vein in the middle. Using a sharp chef's knife, cut the leaves perpendicular to the roll, right up to the central vein; turn the roll around and repeat, discarding the vein. This technique works well for making delicate shreds of basil as well.

Makes 4 servings.

PER SERVING: about II7 cal, I g pro, trace total fat (0 g sat. fat), 30 g carb, 2 g fibre, 0 mg chol, I7 mg sodium, 637 mg potassium. % RDI: 2% calcium, 4% iron, 6% vit A, I37% vit C, I2% folate.

In-Season Fruits

Like vegetables (see In-Season Vegetables, page 57), fruits are best when you buy and eat them at their optimal ripeness. Here are all the details you need to know about when to buy your favourite fruits.

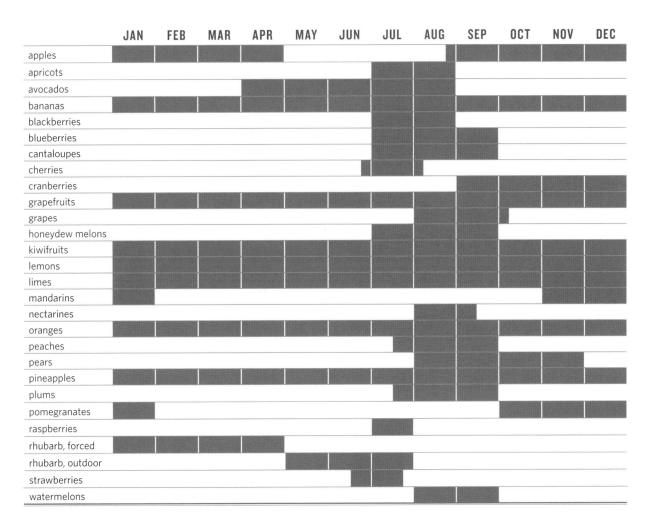

	JAN	FEB	MAR	APR	MAY	JUN	JUL	AUG	SEP	OCT	NOV	DEC
apples	■	■	■	■					■	■	■	■
apricots							■	■				
avocados				■	■							
bananas	■	■	■	■	■	■	■	■	■	■	■	■
blackberries							■	■				
blueberries							■	■				
cantaloupes							■	■				
cherries						■	■					
cranberries									■	■	■	■
grapefruits	■	■	■	■	■	■	■	■	■			
grapes							■	■	■	■		
honeydew melons							■	■				
kiwifruits	■	■	■	■	■	■	■	■	■	■	■	■
lemons	■	■	■	■	■	■	■	■	■	■	■	■
limes	■	■	■	■	■	■	■	■	■	■	■	■
mandarins	■	■									■	■
nectarines							■	■	■			
oranges	■	■	■	■	■	■	■	■				
peaches							■	■	■			
pears							■	■	■	■	■	■
pineapples	■	■	■	■	■	■	■	■	■	■		
plums							■	■				
pomegranates	■	■								■	■	■
raspberries							■					
rhubarb, forced	■	■	■	■								
rhubarb, outdoor					■	■	■					
strawberries						■	■					
watermelons							■	■	■			

MANGO MELON SALAD

LIME JUICE AND HONEY GIVE A SWEET-TART ACCENT TO THIS SALAD OF JUICY, RIPE MANGO
AND TWO KINDS OF MELON. MAKE IT AT THE HEIGHT OF SUMMER, WHEN LOCAL CANTALOUPES
AND WATERMELONS ARE AVAILABLE—THEIR FLAVOUR IS UNPARALLELED.

257

METHOD

In large microwaveable bowl, stir lime juice with honey; microwave on high for 30 seconds. Whisk until honey is dissolved. Let cool.

Add mango, cantaloupe, watermelon, pine nuts (if using) and mint; toss to coat.

INGREDIENTS

3 tbsp	lime juice
3 tbsp	liquid honey
2 cups	cubed (½ inch/1 cm) peeled pitted mango (see how-to, below)
2 cups	cubed (½ inch/1 cm) peeled seeded cantaloupe
2 cups	cubed (½ inch/1 cm) seedless watermelon
¼ cup	pine nuts (optional), toasted (see how-to, page 133)
1 tbsp	shredded fresh mint (see how-to, page 254)

HOW TO

EASILY CUT A MANGO

Cut off the stem end of the mango to make bottom flat. Using a vegetable peeler, peel off half of the skin. Holding the peeled side with a paper towel to prevent slipping, peel the opposite side. Stand the mango on its flat bottom, then cut the flesh off each wide side down to, but avoiding, the pit. Lay the slices on a cutting board; chop, slice or cube.

Makes 4 to 6 servings.

PER EACH OF 6 SERVINGS: about 103 cal, 1 g pro, trace total fat (trace sat. fat), 27 g carb, 2 g fibre, 0 mg chol, 12 mg sodium. % RDI: 2% calcium, 4% iron, 43% vit A, 65% vit C, 10% folate.

FRUIT SALAD
with orange syrup

STEEPING THE ORANGE PEEL IN SIMPLE SYRUP GIVES A SUBTLE CITRUSY NOTE TO THIS SALAD.
THE RECIPE MAKES A LARGE NUMBER OF SERVINGS, SO IT'S IDEAL FOR POTLUCKS AND OTHER GET-TOGETHERS.

INGREDIENTS

4	mangoes, peeled, pitted and chopped (see how-to, page 257)
4	kiwifruit, peeled and chopped
Half	cantaloupe, peeled, seeded and chopped
2 cups	green grapes, halved
1	pineapple, peeled, cored and chopped

Orange Syrup:

1	orange
¼ cup	granulated sugar

METHOD

Orange Syrup: Using vegetable peeler, peel zest off orange in strips; set aside. Halve orange; squeeze juice into glass measure to make ⅓ cup. Set aside.

In small saucepan, bring sugar and ¼ cup water to boil over medium heat, stirring just until dissolved, about 1 minute. Remove from heat. Stir in orange zest; let stand for 10 minutes. Discard zest. Stir in reserved orange juice.

In large bowl, stir together mangoes, kiwifruit, cantaloupe, grapes and pineapple. Toss with orange syrup. Cover and refrigerate for 1 hour before serving. *(Make-ahead: Refrigerate for up to 8 hours.)*

Makes 12 to 16 servings.

PER EACH OF 16 SERVINGS: about 93 cal, 1 g pro, trace total fat (trace sat. fat), 24 g carb, 2 g fibre, 0 mg chol, 5 mg sodium, 266 mg potassium. % RDI: 2% calcium, 2% iron, 10% vit A, 88% vit C, 10% folate.

Scrumptious Shortcakes
for Fruit Salads

OUR FINEST BUTTERMILK SCONES

A classic plain scone like this one can play many roles: a snack with tea or coffee, a slightly sweet sidekick for soups or stews, or a tasty base for fruit shortcakes. Don't feel limited to strawberries and cream—any luscious fruit salad makes an excellent partner.

2½ cups	all-purpose flour
2 tbsp	granulated sugar
2½ tsp	baking powder
½ tsp	baking soda
½ tsp	salt
½ cup	cold butter, cubed
1 cup	buttermilk
1	egg

In bowl, whisk together flour, sugar, baking powder, baking soda and salt. Using pastry blender or two knives, cut in butter until in coarse crumbs. Whisk buttermilk with egg; add to flour mixture, stirring with fork to make soft dough.

Turn out onto lightly floured surface; knead gently 10 times. Pat out into 10- x 7-inch (25 x 18 cm) rectangle; trim edges to straighten. Cut into six squares; cut each diagonally in half.

Place, 1 inch (2.5 cm) apart, on parchment paper–lined rimmed baking sheet. Bake in 400°F (200°C) oven until golden, 12 to 15 minutes. Let cool on pan on rack.

Makes 12 scones.
PER SCONE: about 189 cal, 4 g pro, 9 g total fat (5 g sat. fat), 23 g carb, I g fibre, 37 mg chol, 289 mg sodium. % RDI: 6% calcium, 9% iron, 8% vit A, 26% folate.

MINI LEMON SCONES

These tiny scones are perfect topped with a spoonful of sweet fruit salad and whipped cream. For the fluffiest texture, avoid overmixing and overkneading.

2½ cups	all-purpose flour
2 tbsp	granulated sugar
1 tbsp	grated lemon zest
2½ tsp	baking powder
½ tsp	each baking soda and salt
½ cup	cold unsalted butter, cubed
1 cup	buttermilk
1	egg

Topping:

1	egg, lightly beaten
2 tsp	granulated sugar

In large bowl, whisk together flour, sugar, lemon zest, baking powder, baking soda and salt. Using pastry blender or two knives, cut in butter until in coarse crumbs. Whisk buttermilk with egg; add to flour mixture, stirring with fork to make soft dough.

Turn out onto floured surface; knead gently 10 times. Pat out into scant ¾-inch (2 cm) thick round. Using floured 1¾-inch (4.5 cm) round or fluted cookie cutter, cut out rounds, patting out and cutting scraps twice. Place on parchment paper–lined rimmed baking sheet.

Topping: Brush tops with egg; sprinkle with sugar. Bake in 400°F (200°C) oven just until golden, about 12 minutes. Let cool on pan on rack. *(Make-ahead: Store in airtight container for up to 24 hours.)*

Makes 24 scones.
PER SCONE: about 98 cal, 2 g pro, 5 g total fat (3 g sat. fat), II g carb, trace fibre, 26 mg chol, 122 mg sodium, 36 mg potassium. % RDI: 3% calcium, 5% iron, 4% vit A, 10% folate.

WATERMELON SALAD

FRESH, JUICY WATERMELON TOSSED WITH CRISP FENNEL AND SHAVINGS OF SHARP
ROMANO CHEESE MAKES A WONDERFUL SWEET-AND-SAVOURY SALAD. TRY IT
AS A SIDE DISH WITH YOUR FAVOURITE GRILLED MEAT.

260

INGREDIENTS

1 tbsp	white wine vinegar
1 tbsp	extra-virgin olive oil
Pinch	each salt and pepper
2 cups	seeded cubed watermelon
2 cups	diced cored fennel bulb
1	green onion, thinly sliced
2 tbsp	shaved Romano cheese (about 30 g)

METHOD

In large bowl, whisk together vinegar, oil, salt and pepper.

Add watermelon, fennel and green onion. Toss gently to coat; top with Romano cheese.

You're only using 2 cups of cubed watermelon for this salad, so what to do with all those luscious leftover cubes? Freeze a few handfuls and blend them into frosty smoothies or cocktails, or juice them and make a refreshing twist on pink lemonade. For kids, purée the fruit (with or without additions) and pour into ice pop moulds for a summertime treat you can feel good about.

Makes 4 servings.

PER SERVING: about 95 cal, 3 g pro, 6 g total fat (2 g sat. fat), 9 g carb, 2 g fibre, 7 mg chol, 109 mg sodium, 282 mg potassium. % RDI: 10% calcium, 4% iron, 6% vit A, 20% vit C, 8% folate.

Acknowledgments

Salads are made of disparate but equally important elements, all working in sync. They're the perfect metaphor for a group of people with a variety of skills all working together in harmony toward one beautiful, common end—this book.

As always, the first people I want to thank for their inspired recipes and commitment to great food are our Food director, **Annabelle Waugh,** and her team in The Canadian Living Test Kitchen: **Rheanna Kish, Irene Fong, Amanda Barnier, Jennifer Bartoli** and **Leah Kuhne.** They create and fine-tune every Tested-Till-Perfect recipe that comes out of The Test Kitchen with passion and skill. They make cooking (and editing cookbooks) a pleasure.

Next, thanks to our amazing art director, **Colin Elliott,** who always comes up with fresh ideas for beautiful designs. He's a whiz with graphics and typography, a sharp wit and so fun to work with.

Thanks to the brilliant photographers and stylists who took such luscious pictures of these salads. I'm grateful to photographers **Jeff Coulson** and **Edward Pond,** food stylist **Nicole Young,** and prop stylists **Catherine Doherty** and **Madeleine Johari** for the beautiful images they created especially for this book. Their work and that of many other talented photographers and stylists (see page 270 for a complete list) captured the freshness and creativity of these dishes.

A big thanks to our fabulous copy editor, **Lisa Fielding,** for making sure every detail was just perfect. Any errors are mine, not hers. My gratitude also goes to our indispensable indexer, **Beth Zabloski,** who whipped up the handy index so you can find what you're looking for, and to **Sharyn Joliat** of Info Access, who analyzed each recipe for its nutrient content.

Merci beaucoup to the team at Transcontinental Books: vice-president **Marc Laberge,** publishing director **Mathieu de Lajartre** and assistant editor **Céline Comtois.** They make magic behind the scenes so we can create gorgeous books.

Finally, I would like to offer my sincerest thanks to *Canadian Living*'s acting vice-president and group publisher, **Carlos Lamadrid;** associate publisher, **Susan Antonacci;** and editor-in-chief, **Jennifer Reynolds.** Their love of good food and great books made this project possible.

Tina Anson Mine
project editor

INDEX

CANADIAN LIVING • 150 ESSENTIAL SALADS

263

⬎ = Vegetarian

264

❧ = Vegetarian

Our **Tested-Till-Perfect** guarantee means we've tested every recipe, using the same grocery store ingredients and household appliances as you do, until we're sure you'll get perfect results at home.

ABOUT OUR NUTRITION INFORMATION

To meet nutrient needs each day, moderately active women 25 to 49 need about 1,900 calories, 51 g protein, 261 g carbohydrate, 25 to 35 g fibre and not more than 63 g total fat (21 g saturated fat). Men and teenagers usually need more. Canadian sodium intake of approximately 3,500 mg daily should be reduced, whereas the intake of potassium from food sources should be increased to 4,700 mg per day.

Percentage of recommended daily intake (% RDI) is based on the values used for Canadian food labels for calcium, iron, vitamins A and C, and folate.

Figures are rounded off. They are based on the first ingredient listed when there is a choice and do not include optional ingredients or those with no specified amounts.

ABBREVIATIONS
cal = calories
pro = protein
carb = carbohydrate
sat. fat = saturated fat
chol = cholesterol

269

 = Vegetarian

Credits

RECIPES
All recipes developed by
The Canadian Living Test Kitchen.

PHOTOGRAPHY
Ryan Brook: page 245.

Jeff Coulson: front and back covers; pages 5 (portrait), 6, 7, 8, 9, 11, 14, 18, 34, 35, 42, 47, 60, 61, 69, 75, 77, 85, 93, 100, 101, 108, 112, 113, 115, 119, 131, 138, 139, 142, 147, 164, 165, 169, 173, 176, 186, 190, 194, 195, 201, 208, 213, 214, 215, 220, 229, 232, 233 and 261.

Yvonne Duivenvoorden: pages 21, 23, 30, 41, 58, 96, 105, 122, 126, 135, 151, 160, 163, 181, 185, 225, 240 and 256.

Joe Kim: pages 27 and 145.

Jim Norton: pages 81 and 154.

Edward Pond: pages 38, 54, 65, 72, 111, 217, 236 and 246.

Jodi Pudge: pages 51, 89, 182 and 252.

David Scott: page 248.

FOOD STYLING
David Grenier: pages 47, 75, 131, 245 and 261.

Adele Hagan: pages 42 and 85.

Ian Muggridge: page 252.

Lucie Richard: pages 23, 30, 51, 105, 151, 163, 240, 248 and 256.

Claire Stubbs: pages 21, 38, 41, 58, 72, 77, 81, 89, 93, 96, 135, 142, 160, 181, 182, 185, 225, 236 and 246.

Melanie Stuparyk: pages 27, 69, 108 and 145.

Nicole Young: front and back covers (food); pages 6, 7, 8, 9, 11, 14, 18, 34, 35, 54, 60, 61, 65, 100, 101, 111, 112, 113, 115, 119, 122, 126, 138, 139, 147, 154, 164, 165, 169, 173, 176, 186, 190, 194, 195, 201, 208, 213, 214, 215, 217, 220, 229, 232 and 233.

PROP STYLING
Laura Branson: pages 42, 85, 151, 154, 240 and 252.

Catherine Doherty: front and back covers (food); pages 6, 7, 8, 9, 11, 14, 18, 21, 23, 34, 35, 41, 47, 60, 61, 75, 77, 89, 100, 101, 112, 113, 115, 119, 122, 126, 131, 135, 138, 139, 142, 147, 164, 165, 169, 173, 176, 182, 186, 190, 194, 195, 201, 208, 213, 214, 215, 220, 225, 229, 232, 233 and 261.

Marc-Philippe Gagné: page 105.

Madeleine Johari: 54, 65, 69, 81, 93, 108, 111 and 217.

Maggi Jones: page 246.

Karen Kirk: pages 27, 145 and 245.

Oksana Slavutych: pages 30, 72, 96, 160, 163, 181, 185, 236, 248 and 256.

Genevieve Wiseman: pages 38, 51 and 58.